If You Let Him

Alysia Jackson

Fulton Books
Meadville, PA

Published by Fulton Books 2024

ISBN 979-8-88982-789-4 (paperback)
ISBN 979-8-88982-790-0 (digital)

CONTENTS

DEDICATION

I want to dedicate this book to several people in my life that have kept me strong, and taught me who I truly want to strive to be, starting with my husband. You are the reason I wanted to pursue my relationship with God in the first place. You made me feel alive, and a different kind of encouragement and source of freedom I had never felt in my life before. Your love encouraged me to be myself and explore everything God has in this life for me. You showed me responses that I had never seen in my lifetime until we met that left me speechless and confused such as patience, loyalty, understanding, and true love. The way you responded to the parts of me that were not worthy of love, and the patient ways you helped me understand that I could let go of my fears, hardness in my heart, and defense mechanisms, were beautiful. The way you nurtured me when I needed it most, and the ways you spoke of faith did nothing but encourage me, and for once in my entire life make me feel secure, safe, protected, respected, precious, and loved just for being me. You gave me security that whatever came our way, or whatever leftover hurt buried deep came out of me, you would be there to love it away. All of this was so intriguing to me, that I didn't know what to do with it, and sometimes still don't. I love you, and appreciate you for all that you are, for saving me, for never giving up on me, for giving me a life I look forward to every day, and a friendship and bond that means the world to me. I can't imagine life without you, and I don't want to.

I also want to thank my children who have always been my reason for trying harder in life, and many times all I felt I had to live for. For always being a hug and kiss when I needed it, or a word of encouragement to know I was doing my best. I am very proud of you both, and who you are, and being your mother has always been a blessing. Thank you for understanding me, and understanding what I went through to ensure you were taken care of, and especially understanding when I didn't get it right. Thank you for standing by my side and always loving me, I love you, and will always be here for you, always.

Lastly, I want to thank my bonus momma. I am not always easy to deal with, and definitely find myself needing help and guidance in this life and nowhere else to turn. I want to thank you for always being a true and honest listening ear, who has had nothing but great intentions for me and my life. Thank you for the many talks we have had, and always making me feel better, stronger, and even normal afterwards. Thank you for never judging me and loving me as your own. You have also taught me so much about what a true relationship with God can do in my life. You are an inspiration to me, a wonderful friend, and one of my greatest blessings. I love you more than I can say.

There are many others along the way I have been so blessed to come in contact with, some are mentioned in this book. I cannot list everyone, but you know who you are. Thank you for any positive light you have provided my life. One thing about me is I will never forget it. I pray to have the opportunity to continue writing and show many more ways that God works through people to encourage others, never forget that you can be used to help others find God and their true purpose too, if you let Him!

INTRODUCTION

Serve wholeheartedly, as if you were serving the
Lord, not people.

—Ephesians 6:7

Everyone is so selfish. That's what I heard today when I was asking why I was so sad all day long. I haven't felt the same kind
of peace the last week or so no matter what I did. Tried relaxing,
tried thinking about all the things I love to do so much, tried to
do them, and still nothing. When my soul finally felt completely
drained today, I thought why bother any more.

People truly only think about themselves. As I numbly answered
text messages and emails about fixing and doing things for other people to help with their issues that are more important than anything
right now, after waiting all week long, they felt it necessary to wait
until I get a break which is so needed from everything they already
demand from me every day, suddenly now barking at me to fix them.
Thank you?

No regard for the fact you have a family, too, or may need a
break from questions, concerns, arguments, or every thought all week
long. It's my problem, but I need you to fix it now! So many requests,
you can't keep up, but you smile. You stop doing what you're doing
mid thought to help them. Like a zombie, you put them first until
you have nothing left for anyone or anything else including yourself.
Have you ever felt this pressure at work, at home, or in any aspect
of life? Talk about intense. Everywhere you go, you can see or feel

selfishness if you think about it, including your own. Dang, Lord, for real. Okay, that was one way to lead me here, and you're right. I'm constantly staring at people astonished by how selfish they can be while feeling sorry for myself that I must listen or help nonstop. And I care, I really do. But when people don't care about you or what you say or do, and even talk about you behind your back, you wonder if they even care about the great lengths you go in order to serve them, keep everyone sane and happy as can be, at your own expense.

When everyone turns on you here and there at some point, depending upon what you do or don't do for them, or how they feel about whether it's good or not.

I guess You do know how that feels, Lord, don't You? I tell people all the time you must suffer to grow, and then selfishly, I ask God for the pain to stop for me.

Lord, I feel like it just won't stop. I love and I give, and I deplete myself to do it, only to encounter nothing but takers. Takers that leave me wondering if and when they'll do it if they haven't yet.

Scared to get too close to anyone or anything because people are either taking from me mentally or wasting my time. Time I need to refill myself again just to gain enough strength back to cater to the needs of the world again, never having time to enjoy myself. Every thought consumed with trying to prevent getting hit in the head all the time by the disgruntlement of others.

Why do we have to treat each other like this? Lord, I'm so confused. Why do they make things up about me and each other? Lord, that isn't even true, or they heard it that way because they wanted to, or because they said it once that way in the past, or just to get what they wanted in the first place? Why are my parents both so selfish? Sometimes I just want to wash my hands of trying with them until after some time passes, and I feel compelled to try again a little at a time.

One of them can physically only care about herself and making sure the world agrees with her, or she's done talking to you, because her way will forever be the only way. Even though everything she does is wrong, way wrong, no normal person would debate me on this, I promise.

To the other one that doesn't have enough communication skills to send a "happy birthday" text, or even an "I'm sorry, I missed it" when you put it on their lap with a bow.

Then the family lines continue. The people out there in this world continue wandering around like they are the only person that matters on this earth. Everyone else is just here to serve them. Even if you aren't as bad as those people, if you think about it, I'm sure you have a little selfishness in you, or maybe even a lot. It's all whether you know it or not, recognize it or not, deny it or not, or just ignore it.

In two sermons the last few weeks from different sources, I heard do you love God for the blessings He can give you, for the promise of heaven if you're faithful, or do you love Him because of what He's already done for you, or what you expect Him to do for you right now? Or do you love Him because He's with you to strengthen and protect you and comfort you no matter what time of the day it is, no matter what your location, status, gender, weight, personality, looks, whatever because He created you and everything about your life and loves you unconditionally?

I think if we're honest with ourselves, we can say we ask for things a lot. Things I think sometimes we even know we have no business asking for. Things we want to have happen in our lives, and maybe even get mad at when He doesn't give them to us. I definitely have. But the more I learn about how He can give me way better than what I want, I start to remind myself to say, "If that's in your plans, Lord, or what You want to do with me" because I don't want to short myself.

Story after story in the Bible if you truly read them, if you consider the person wrote each story on their own experience, it's all too real. A woman so desperate to be a mother, she chooses to please her husband by having a son as God told him he would. When she thought she was standing in the way of His blessing, she let him sleep with her handmaiden and watched her carry her husband's child. Could you do that, ladies? Most of us start snarling when a female gets too close to our man. I know I do. Just for her to eventually get pregnant with their son too a bit later. Her plan was nowhere near as good as God's. She had to let Him work. She had to practice faith in the pathway. She had to let Him.

I have to stop thinking about what I want to see at the end of my life and know what He has planned will be better than even that. If I can let Him.

It may mean I have to put up with a lot of selfish people. Our enemy is truly always working against us. Think about your recent thoughts about yourself and about others that weren't good. Do you think God, who is love, would put those in your head? How many times have you been concerned about something someone else said? How many times have you been shocked about something you found to be true about someone? Something they did or said? This happens to me all the time. They let the enemy's thoughts take over their mind. Can you recognize it because you've done the same in order to know it's done, or instead had your heart broken realizing something someone has said about you?

This is how we are all out here living with each other, and it has to stop. We create so much of our own issues, but the cycle can be stopped. How does that happen?

It happens by staying close to God daily. These thoughts were my very own this morning. Even after years of working on how to get closer to God and hear the soul and the spirit He has placed inside me and each and every one of us that we unknowingly suppress each and every day.

Because life is hard, people are hard. I know this firsthand not only being around very hard people most of my life, but also being hard myself for most of my own life. We hurt ourselves and each other. To top it off, there's a crew of evil all around, talking us into believing and doing horrible things that are easier to do, but getting us in a whole lot of trouble and making us feel mad, empty, sad, alone, or guilty, and they're everywhere.

Sounds like just following God and giving Him all your worries and cares is something someone made up that was just tired of caring, and it truly does. But you won't understand it unless you truly get there, or are trying to every day, because that's what it takes. He gives you peace because He gives you the answers if you listen, if you let Him. It's easier to be selfish, mad, angry, sad, alone, miserable, and complain about it.

It's a lot harder to give up yourself, your desires, your selfishness, and love people who don't deserve it because God wants you to. But if that's what you follow and you really want to please Him, you will. Imagine if we all did. That sounds like heaven. No misunderstanding or hurting each other. True grace and understanding. The answers and guidance on everything we need spoke directly into our spirits.

I came to this book by making a commitment I would try hard to know who Jesus was, and I got much more than I ever could have imagined. I knew very little of God. Because of all the things I had been through in my life, I had a deep inability to trust or get close to people, let alone God.

My journey is right before your eyes literally as I write like a kindergartner that doesn't know how to even find a scripture in the Bible to being given responses to my questions, and led to a lot of healing and even thankfulness for those things because of what I learned from them and how my situations can help others learn about the way, the truth, and the light. I read book after book, more intrigued with how to know God, and upset because I didn't already know Him like that. What it could have saved me from if I had. The more I read, the more I felt there was no denying the experiences I was having were from God. Even after four years, I still feel like an elementary-student Christian, but the feeling of the wait will be worth it to graduate in heaven and to make God proud.

The thought of making people happy when they think of me when I'm gone, or for people to say I made a difference in their lives would make going through all of those situations worth it.

God is truly the only way to that life. That life comes with great burden and responsibility.

To lose your own selfishness more and more each blessing you're given. To live an abundant life that was meant just for you, and is who and what you were meant to be.

You only get one life to choose that direction. What do you have to lose? I can assure you that you can ask yourself about all you wish to gain instead.

No matter what you've been through or who you are, period.

I am not claiming to be an expert on God or faith, or a perfect Christian. Quite the contrary. I do not know the Bible or scriptures by heart. I fail all the time. But I have learned that it is normal to fail, and how God can be beside me everywhere I am, teaching me to be better each and every day. More prepared for each challenge life throws at me, with His guidance. These are simply examples of how I learned to talk to Him and to listen to Him and how only He can and has changed my life in wonderful ways.

If I let Him.

CHAPTER 1

The Deep Darkness

Looking back at the chain of events of my sister's and I's lives growing up, and all the things we went through is honestly scary and tormenting. We both went through everything you could honestly think of from abandonment, lack of education, suicide attempts, extreme poverty, and physical, mental, verbal, and sexual abuse. We lacked basic needs, guidance, and experiences as children. We still discover situations that we find eerily bone-chilling and crazy when we talk about them and piece them together from our individual perspectives to create a web that does not feel real at times. We had no idea how much darkness and evil lurked around every corner of our lives while we were in them. Evil eventually worked to separate us, and for well over ten years, we didn't even speak to each other. Evil preyed on us everywhere we went like vulnerable sheep unattended, because we were. No parents to guide us and the half of our parents that we did have present allowed and even created and encouraged the evil into our lives. Looking back, the only way I can explain it was a deep darkness that only comes with great sorrow in the rearview mirror.

I say all of that to say that if I can learn how to find God through the aftermath of that deep darkness and begin to travel on the narrow road, truly anyone can. That does not mean you are perfect. Lord definitely knows I have to stay close to Him and refill myself every day in this fallen world. But knowing how I felt inside eventually after the deep darkness became too much, events stacking up on top of each other like Satan had it out for us, and the person it turned me into, I would never have ever guessed I could be who I am today, and have the thoughts and relationship with God that I do today.

I have done and said many things in life that I am definitely not proud of. I'm sure most can relate. You may, just like I did, be thinking there is no way you can overcome your situation, there is no way God could love me like all the gospel songs and books say He does, or that it's just all BS.

That's exactly what I was beginning to think as my world grew darker and darker each day. Anyone who knew who I was before I'm sure would be all too quick to point out and attest to the person that I was. I said exactly how I felt no matter how it felt to you. I've held knives up to people to protect myself. I've hurt myself. I've jumped out of moving vehicles to fight people, took crap from no one, and made it obvious that I wouldn't dare you to try. I've definitely had a tongue that could slash you into many pieces, and that's just scratching the surface. Later realizing these were all just defense mechanisms for the deep darkness that was normal for me, for us, until recently.

I numbly went about my life as each event seemed to take my soul. I told my husband in the beginning when he started expressing interest in me that I am definitely not who he wants. I told him there's nothing special about me, I have no gifts, God doesn't talk to me, I'm way too broken and ruthless for him, and just too much to handle. I told him this because of how wonderful of a person he is and was, as a warning to abort this mission before getting demolished.

Thankfully, he was faithful, and very, very persistent. His love for God first and then for me began my transformation into a world that I pray everyone has a means to find themselves one day.

A journey of a thousand miles begins with just one step.

CHAPTER 2

One Step

*Sometime in 2020 before I started
putting dates on my writing*

I made a commitment to myself to sit down and learn about God and get to know Him. I had no idea how or what would even come of it. But I saw my husband's family and how full of faith and joy they were, and the more I heard about this peace that only God could provide, I was on a mission. With peaceful people in my life for the first time ever, the opportunity presented itself for me to have great thoughts and to think about what I truly wanted for my life.

I had random thoughts as I read through my Bible, trying to understand what exactly the stipulations of this relationship with God are, and even more randomly something was guiding me to the answers with my own thoughts on where to go, learning about His word on the way. I had no idea in the moment that God was working through me with the spirit He placed inside me, inside all of us that we have to find.

These are the first notes I took in my journal as I started to read the Bible from the beginning, recording random scriptures along the way I felt would be helpful. Some scriptures so random, I am not sure what they even meant to me in the moment now looking back. Watch my faith and knowledge grow stronger before your very eyes, and the essential process of the evolution of my relationship developing with God that is continuous even today, as I strive to turn in to who God truly created me to be. This was a long journey, and continues to be. Stay with me, and trust the process.

Lord, I look to you for everything I need in my life. Help me put all my expectations in you. "To my soul, wait silently for God alone, for my expectation is from him" (Psalm 62:5 KJV). "He is my rock and my salvation, He is my defense; I shall not be moved."

"How great does that sound?" I remember saying to myself.

Second Timothy 2:14: "Keep reminding God's people of these things. Warn them before God against quarreling about words; it is of no value, and only ruins those who listen."

Second Timothy 2:20–21: "In a large house there are articles not only of gold and silver, but also of wood and clay; some are for special purposes and some for common use. Those who cleanse themselves from the latter will be instruments for special purposes, made holy, useful to the Master and prepared to do any good work."

In 2 Timothy 2:22, evil desires of youth—it's okay to be calm, rid yourself of young evils. The Lord's servants must not be quarrelsome. The Bible predicts the future back then? "This know also, that in the last days, perilous times shall come. For men shall be lovers of their own selves, covetous, boasters, proud, blasphemers, disobedient to parents, unthankful, unholy, without natural affection, trucebreakers, false accusers, incontinent, fierce, despisers of those that are good, traitors, heady, highminded, lovers of pleasure more than lovers of God" (2 Timothy 3:1–5 KJV). Doesn't that sound familiar? How could you not be intrigued and believe? How could you not be intrigued and believe? Believers must hold tight and stay away from "those people" described. Says preach the word in every season. You will be calm upon death. Your fight for God is over. God will then crown you and everyone else who longed for His appearance.

So Jesus has genealogy—who knew?

Abraham, Isaac, Jacob, Judah, Perez, Hezron, RAM, Amminindab, Nashon, Salmon and Rahab, Boaz and Ruth, Obed, Jesse, King David, Solomon, Rehoboam, Abijah, Asa, Jehoshaphat, Jehoram, Uzziah, Jotham, Ahaz, Hezekiah, Manasseh, Josiah,

Jeconiah, Shealtiel, Zerubbabel, Abihud, Eliakim, Azor, Zadok, Akim, Elihud, Eleazar, Matthan, Jacob, Joseph (married Mary).

Several of those names sound familiar.

John the Baptist baptized Jesus in the Jordan River, and many other people as well. When he baptized Jesus, heaven parted and he saw the Spirit of God. Jesus fasted forty days and forty nights. And the devil tempted Him, saying, "Just turn those stones into bread if you're so hungry." Jesus responded, "Man cannot live on bread alone, but on every word that comes from God's mouth."

Jesus was preaching in Syria. Syria! This is where my grandfather's family is from!

God forgives your sins when you pray and forgive others of their sins.

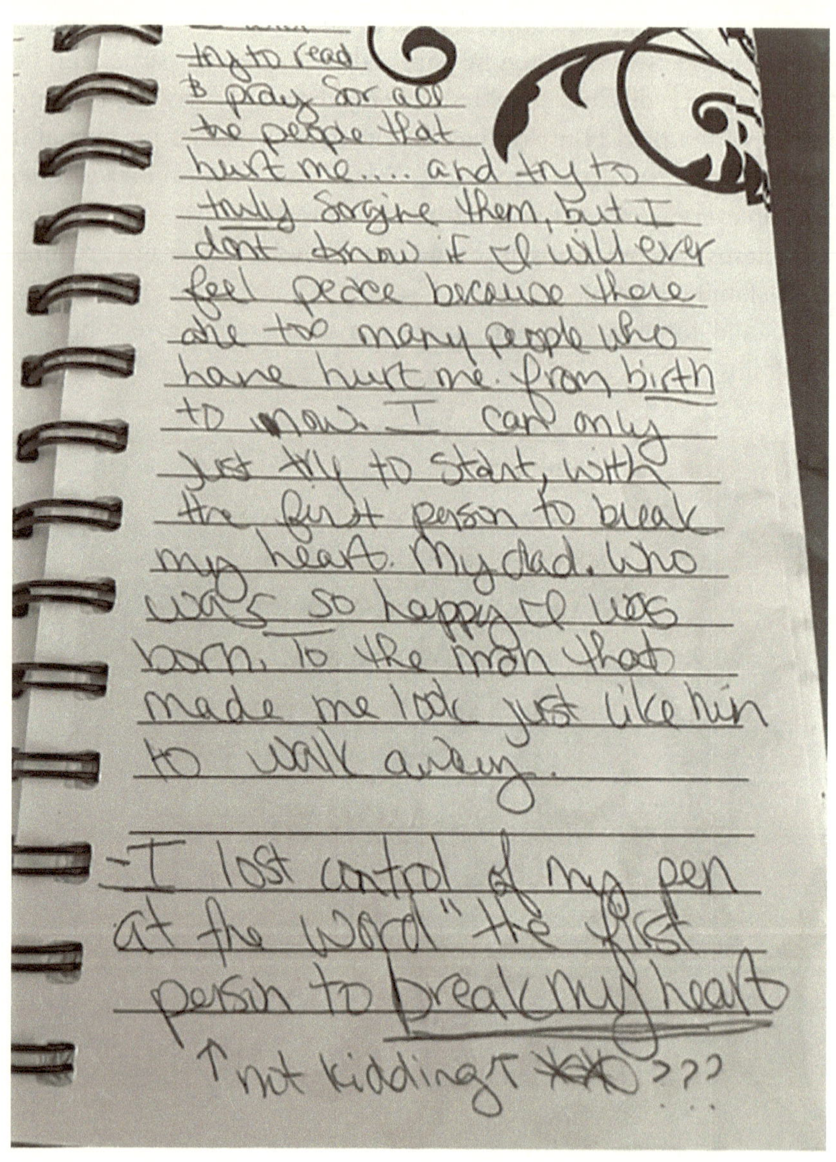
try to read
& pray for all
the people that
hurt me..... and try to
truly forgive them, but I
don't know if I will ever
feel peace because there
are too many people who
have hurt me. From birth
to now. I can only
just try to start, with
the first person to break
my heart. My dad. Who
was so happy I was
born. To the man that
made me look just like him
to walk away.

- I lost control of my pen
at the word "the first
person to break my heart
↑ not kidding ↑ XX ???

CHAPTER 3

Something Has Happened

May 31, 2020

Ideas pop in my head sometimes now, but they are different from just my ideas.

Today, I saw all the bad people I know that used to be good. I saw a flash of all of them from start to end. It was a timeline that showed where they stepped away from God and how they then got obviously worse and worse. It was intense.

Because I have received the message that forgiveness is so important on this journey, today I will try to read and pray for all the people that hurt me…and try to truly forgive them, but I don't know if I will ever feel peace because there are too many people who have hurt me from birth to now. I can only just try to start, with the first person to break my heart. My dad. Who was so happy I was born. To the man that made me look just like him and to walk away.

(I lost control of my pen at the word "the first person to break my heart." Not kidding!) This was the first experience I had that felt supernatural to me. I wrote the words, pen flying before my eyes, without even knowing what words I wrote until I stopped and read them myself. My hand seemed to be traveling faster than my mind, like it was guided on what to write to reveal it to even me. It was very quick, very shocking, and left me stunned as to what had just happened.

To notice which people stand out, notice Matthew 5:5: "Blessed are the meek for they will inherit the earth." This is why they don't care that they seem meek to the world. They know the secret. This is where I was led in reading right after.

This is me again. I wish for peace every single day, but I just cannot find it. What I want most in my life is to be meek. I have always been solo, alone, but with people physically all around me, people that made me tense. Almost every single one of them. I would think God doesn't talk to me. But now looking back I can see that He was with me. He told me which situations to not be in. But sometimes I knew it was bad but had no choice.

I can't get peace. I can't be meek unless I forgive all of those people, Lord?

Does this also mean I can't care about my body at all? Or my clothes? Shouldn't you take care of yourself for confidence and to be attractive to your partner?

I was led to Matthew 6:24–25: "No man can serve two masters: for either he will hate the one, and love the other, or else he will hold to one, and despise the other. Ye cannot serve God and mammon (riches). Therefore, I say unto you, be not anxious for your life, what ye eat, or what ye shall drink, nor yet for your body, what ye shall put on. Is not the life more than the food, and the body more than the raiment (clothing or garments)? Behold the birds of the heaven, that they sow not, neither do they reap, nor gather into barns; and your heavenly Father feedeth them. Are not ye of much more value than they?" Of course, I had to look up the words I didn't understand along the way, and that is fine. I wanted to know the true meaning of what I was reading.

In this chapter, God goes on to say how He creates all things naturally for His creatures without them having to even worry about it. He ends by stating, "Seek ye first his kingdom, and his righteousness; and all these things shall be added unto you" (verse 33).

Make sure to put the verses in later, because it's important to see where my mind really went, and it can be put back later. Read the back where you went. (This was pressed against my mind hard while writing, so I made a note of it in the back of my book, along with other requests from God along the way, and I did them).

In the back of my notes, I wrote in case I forget, God told me today our time is Saturday morning, early when no one is around. Not Sunday because I don't completely give Him my mind because I feel I am not wanting to give up too much cuddle time.

God said I have always wanted to be an author, to write books. He also said I always wanted to know him. If he teaches me, and I write it down. It's a book that can teach more than just me… OH MY GOD, YES!!! YES I WILL!

My instructions on how to continue seemed to be set for me.

CHAPTER 4

The Undeniable Intervention of God

This was the first experience I had that was completely undeniable with God, where He revealed things about me to me. It was the first time I felt a true connection, that God had spoken to me directly from His spirit within me.

God said I have always wanted to be an author, to write books. He also said I always wanted to know Him. If He teaches me and I write it down, it's a book that can teach more than just me. Oh my God, yes! Yes, I will!

I once again lost control of my pen at the words "write it down." He said write it just like that. Show where He came into my thoughts. Amazing. It was like receiving an offer letter for the most precious gift ever, a dream come true that I had long forgotten about.

I can heal in front of the world. To know how to heal for myself, but also to help others know how to heal.

God said He'd show me my words, but I had to study to keep receiving them. Then all of a sudden, He said read Matthew 7:7: "Ask, and it shall be given to you; seek, and ye shall find; knock, and it shall be opened unto you."

Get an editor—they will put this in order. He said we can do this in several books if we need to. He knows it will take forever, but that it will be my life forever. To teach others, not just me.

I lost control of my pen at "to teach others, not just me." Wow. Again, I was just writing words quicker than I could keep up with and finding out myself what they were after writing them!

Mix pages that are typed and written to show the impact of what you felt when I stepped in, He said. Do not only put the verse, but the entire verse. So people can read on the fly anywhere with the message included. I was writing down direction after direction as it came, as the spirit moved over the pages.

I did not write each page in order. For some reason, I skipped around, but amazingly each paragraph fell to the right place where it was meant to be.

Let the dead bury their own dead? What does that mean?

CHAPTER 5

Lesson 1

June 6, 2020

Matthew 6:30 is the answer. "Will he not much more clothe you? You of little faith." So it doesn't say you can't care about your clothes. It means "I will always give you what you need. Just seek me."

I've worked around people too long. I want to work with You, God.

God immediately pressed into my mind, "Know who the people are. The guy right in front of you in the suit being vibrantly spiritual. Really, really trying too hard. These are not my people. My people are meek. That's who you want to be."

Suddenly I had to run inside, away from the sunshine because a wasp wouldn't leave me alone. Not like normal, up in my face every time I went back out on the porch. Then it disappeared right in front of me. It was too aggressive not to notice, like a stalker having an argument when you say you want nothing to do with them. This lasted so long, I looked outside at my coffee and at the beautiful sun and thought this is punishment.

Relationships feel corporate and sterile where there is division, and chaos is what I heard next.

Blessed are you when people insult you, persecute you, and falsely say all kinds of evil against you because of me. Rejoice and be glad because great is your reward in heaven, for in the same way they persecuted the prophets before you. Say whatever you want about me. I will just do what's right. This came to me right after thinking about how I had scolded some of my coworkers. I felt so bad, and didn't know what words to say to put it back together, I didn't sleep last night over it.

I was led to the pond in my backyard that has the loudest frogs ever, where I was told what words needed to be said. I suddenly felt peace, and all the frogs cheered louder than normal when it sank in. Matthew 6:27: "Which of you by worrying add a single hour to your life."

Matthew 6:34: "Therefore do not worry about tomorrow, for tomorrow will worry about itself. Each day has enough trouble of its own."

Ever notice when you talk to a meek person, you may think they are weak, but you wish you could care less what others thought just like they do? No point for you to judge them, what they wear or how they look, because they don't care, and they are not judging you. So who cares? Imagine if you were meek. You knew the secret, you could talk to God, you didn't care what anyone thought, or you rarely seemed to get upset, seemingly always in control. Because if you did talk to God, He would tell you exactly what to do and say to make everything right again. You are not the suited man having to try really hard. You are yourself, thanking God for always telling you what to say and do that makes life go in your favor, or even better in God's favor, which is even better than we can ever imagine ourselves. It makes you never worry, or learn how to turn worry over to Him. He tells you who to stay away from. He tells you what is really bothering your significant other so you can handle them exactly the way they want to be. It makes them love you even more. It makes them never want to hurt you, could never think of cheating on you, never want to disrespect you. It then makes you as cared for on the flip side, which starts the harmony in your life in every relationship. If you let Him.

Or you don't believe it can happen like this because it just doesn't sound believable. Because you don't know how to listen because you think it means God's voice coming from the sky. So did I!

But I wanted it so bad, I tried all my life to be like the meek. It's not easy to be meek, especially living in and around others who are anything but meek. It is so easy to judge others, to make us feel better about ourselves. Why would they wear that? Why would they do that? Why would they say that? They don't know what they are talking about. I suddenly heard Matthew 7:24: "In the same way you judge others, you will be judged, and with the measure you use, it will be measured to you."

So I am judging and can't be myself because of how much others are judging me, and I am being smothered by it, so I smother them back (and the frogs are silent this time, but the wind blew so hard out of nowhere). You hypocrite. First, take the plank out of your own eye, then you will see clearly to remove the speck from your brother's eye. And I am back to my conclusion from last weekend.

Matthew 7:12: "So in everything you do, do unto others what you would have them do to you. For this sums up the lesson of the law and prophets."

I had been led back to this very verse almost every time I sat down to read. It began to seem like the conclusion of my daily lesson.

CHAPTER 6

What Do I Want My Life to Look Like?

June 13, 2020

Enjoying my vibrant screened porch. Sun coming up, the sky is North Carolina bright blue. I can hear birds everywhere, woodpecker every now and then, frogs sometimes louder than normal. Thinking what could make life perfect?

I heard in my head, what do you want your life to be? Just ask.

Matthew 6:22 says, "Your eyes are the lamp of the body, if your eyes are healthy your whole body is full of light, and if they are unhealthy full of dark." When you are run-down with stress, lack of life, it is easy to be dark and have bad spirits come in. Ensuring you are light and happy keeps you close to God, but your eyes light back up when you are actually close to God. So those with lights in their eyes are good. Those with genuine eyes are good. Matthew 7:14: "Small is the gate and narrow the road that leads to life and how to find it!"

If you find it? How do you get there? Do you know God?

He responded to me again by taking me to scripture Matthew 7:2–23: "Just saying Lord is not enough for heaven. He will say I never knew you, away from the kingdom of heaven."

So how do I know if You know me?

Apostles were given the authority to drive out impure spirits and heal every disease and sickness. Simon (Peter), Andrew, James, John, Philip, Bartholomew, Thomas, Matthew, James, Thaddeus, Simon, Judas. Matthew 11:28: "Come to me all you who are weak and burdened, and I will give you rest. Take my yoke upon you and learn from me for I am gentle and humble in heart, and you will find rest in your souls. For my yoke is easy, and my burden is light."

June 20, 2020

So on the porch again. I lean back and listen to the beautiful sounds of nature. Birds and frogs talking back and forth, but very lightly. Often in the distance to the right, left, middle, back and forth in sync like a concert. While looking at birds soar in the sunrise in the clouds, I think who doesn't love nature? Who could stand to only do hustle and bustle and not be relaxed by nature to regenerate? Then I open my book to the last page I wrote, and it said, "The Lord really does teach if you listen." I felt as though the Lord Himself was telling me I get distracted, but thank You for reminding me to get back on track.

I begin to read as I go to Matthew 10:16: "I am sending you out like sheep amongst wolves." And the once peaceful birds get aggressive. Many will not believe you, but Matthew 10:13–15: "If the home is deserving of your peace rest in it, if it is not let your peace return to you! If anyone will not welcome you or listen to your words, leave that home or town and shake the dust off your feet."

Continue the verse to see what the reward of the meek will be. Very powerful. The end of that verse says, "Verily I say onto you, it shall be more tolerable for the land of Sodom and Gomorrah in the day of judgment, than for that city."

Sounds fairly simple. Do what you do, and keep going if they don't come along with you.

July 7, 2020

I'm reading about dreams in a book called *Destiny Calls* by Norman and Grace Barnes. I read of the amazing things that they had done to help others, and a line hit me. Orphans in India, no parents, and how prevalent it was. Their faces disoriented, isolated, bewildered, and drained of hope. This brought me back to growing up with a father that seemingly abandoned me, and a mother that I had to raise myself rather than be raised by. It also reminded me of all the pictures and videos when I was little where even I thought *what a happy girl* for someone whose soul seemed to be sucked dry already.

Her eyes were hollow, but she tried to love life so hard (pen flapping again, astonished when I read my own sentence).

Someone once told me my granddad, whom I loved and adored, said he had come back to Ohio to make sure I would survive okay after hearing what was going on in my life, and returned to find the last event had changed me for good. He said her soul was gone. He had been called and was told that I was molested at five years old by the man I had told my mother to stop leaving me alone with for many months. He was not all there mentally, which is why I felt bad even saying anything. Even I knew this so young. But this man, who had many mental issues of his own, whose wife had married him because she was a devout Catholic woman and felt bad for him and wanted to just take care of him. A man who didn't seem to know where he was most days, or even know he had crusted lip corners every single day, was my babysitter. My mother thought nothing wrong with this even after being told by me that I was scared of him. That is a small piece of me feeling like an orphan, but all of it combined couldn't come close to living the way those orphans lived. Both parents dead because they were killed? Even if my water or electricity was shut off here and there, we at least had it 80 percent of the time. Beds that were rid of disease. We as Americans blind ourselves of this on purpose and think they could change it themselves, but as basically an orphan myself, I understand who will help you or teach you? This is where the love of God comes into you. Once you know this, what small things you can do to change their world. Can you not help?

The more you read, the more you know your path, but the less you know about your current life. God, I have no passion left for mundane daily tasks when I feel what kind of feelings I do when thinking about helping people to this magnitude.

But when you read all about miracles that happen, how do you know what your part is or how to get started? God told me I had grown bored with mundane tasks because I want to use myself to bring people together and help them to find peace in themselves.

But I can't find peace myself, Lord. How can I teach others peace?

Be baptized? Why? And just me or everyone?

The spirit comes down from heaven as a dove and remains on Him. John 5:1–47. This is mentioned in the Bible as a result of what happens when Jesus is baptized.

To cleanse yourself from baptism to baptism in between. Jesus was just a carpenter of Nazareth if you don't think you know enough. You had fever to be held off for baptism. Do not be afraid of what you had. This was what I heard in reference to myself having the coronavirus and being turned away for a tubal reversal surgery for having the antibody, along with the concerns of what comes along with the virus. Mark 1:29–34 (I had not even made it to reading Mark yet before I was led there). They pour new wine into new wineskins, and both are preserved. God was seemingly telling me before I could get pregnant, He expected me to be baptized during the coronavirus when churches were closed.

CHAPTER 7

When Life Gets in the Way

August 9, 2020

Hey, God, I wanted to visit more this week, but this was a little more painful than I thought it would be. Can we talk? You said only the ones that can hear You are Yours, they will be led by their shepherd. How can I hear You all the time?

You don't know the hour of my return because you should be ready for it at any time. From everyone who has been given much, much more will be asked.

August 15, 2020

Which way do I go, God? Work suddenly went from on the way to being great and calm to coming back to the world is on fire and keeps getting worse. What is the right decision, Lord? Help me. I need to know how to get things back on track. I have choices to make that will make or break me and this building. I need to know what to do. Should I go with this one or that one? And how do I fix this?

This was my cry for help during a very challenging situation, in a very challenging position, in an extremely challenging industry, which put me through the wringer for a very long time, until God changed my season.

I am led to a place in my Bible where it says, "When you ask the Holy Spirit to give you ears to hear and eyes to see, God will open His treasure house and give you fresh insight into His parables."

My mother-in-law, or bonus momma as we say, was pressed to my heart right at that moment, and I suddenly felt that I needed to call her immediately. She listened and told me exactly what I had been drawn to in the Bible. Ask God to let you see with your eyes and hear with your ears. Show up each day and ask God to show you which decision is the right one to help you. It was as if God placed her in my mind, and gave her the thoughts to confirm what He had placed in me.

August 22, 2020

For some reason, this morning I was told to go through my writing from the beginning. This last month had been so hard. First, I got COVID-19 the day before my tubal reversal surgery. We were so excited that morning. I felt like I was having really bad sinus issues, which is normal for me. My COVID-19 test was negative before, and now waiting in the room for them to give my husband discharge instructions, they suddenly came in, three of them, and said I was positive for the antibody. How? They immediately sent me to get tested. They said I could come back when I can take another negative test. Devastated and scared, we went for me to take a test. This was my second one. The first one didn't hurt. This one burned in my nose so bad, and I knew. We went home and tried to continue loving and taking care of our kids cautiously. They assumed I had just had surgery. Two days later, the positive results were delivered to me with basically "good luck" instructions. Don't know anything about it. Stay home. Now my headache was at its peak. Inside my nose all the way up to my head was burning. My legs ached so bad, I went to my treadmill one night at 4:00 a.m. But I couldn't do it because of my head, nose, and lack of breath. Each morning, a different child had a fever and headache. Thankfully they were usually better after twenty-four hours. We never told them what they had at that moment. Just gave the medicine like any other flu and kept everyone inside, until we went in the heat one day, and my nose and head got worse. I couldn't breathe well.

One day, I got a call asking me questions from the health department and had to sign a document stating if I left the house, I could be charged with a misdemeanor. To go back to work, I now have to have a negative test. Going in for the test, they tell me people are still showing positive eight to nine weeks after symptoms. They send me a letter that says I haven't had any more symptoms and I can go back to work, but my test is positive. I go back to work after this hell for two weeks of being scared, of what could happen if I took a ride in the car. To what if this never goes away, what if I have long-term damages, to I don't want to give this to anyone else!

My struggle continued when I came back to work, and everyone was asking about my time off, and I was very short with them to avoid contact. Those that were there were obviously upset that I was off, especially while being so short-staffed with nothing but COVID-19 scares. People quitting or going on medical leaves all around, stress was getting higher. My rescheduled surgery was only a few more weeks ahead. I had to work fast. Even though I worked hard for a solid plan for the week of my absence, when it went smooth because of all my efforts up front to set them up for success and relieve some pressure, everyone assumed it was obviously because I was gone. Now I'm taking another week off for what seems like pleasure. How could I?

Awaiting on yet another COVID-19 test result that would determine our fate on surgery or no surgery, yet again my husband and I couldn't be too excited just yet. After attempting to spend some time alone together the weekend before for a much-needed break, I took him to the beach. When my reservation was canceled the Friday we should check in, they put me somewhere else on the fly. Upon arriving, I realized this was cheaper but nowhere near as nice. I knew he knew it, too, but I just tried to stay positive. When the place was packed, we knew this could be dangerous. Kids everywhere and so many people, we couldn't swim in the lazy river or the pool. As much as I love the ocean, I couldn't even swim. The water was so dirty. We kept to ourselves in the room, and when I got back, I started not to feel so great again. Calling the day before surgery as the clinic was about to close, they told me I was negative. I was sure in my mind I had it again, or would just be positive from the first time since it was only about four weeks ago.

We prayed to be able to have the surgery because it would be so long before I would be able to reschedule time off from work again. If this was in God's plan, it was going to have to happen now. My symptoms had went away, and my test was negative. After a long week of recovering from a surgery, that was a bit more intense than I imagined in my mind, only the thought of the joy we could share as husband and wife and as a family didn't really let me think about the pain. Still very fuzzy, I went back to work the next Monday. Back to everyone thinking "here comes the cause of this mess." The fact that I had tried to help everyone to the fullest of my extent meant nothing.

This reminded me of so many things going on now. As we all hate about politics, religion, and race, we are only seeing our own side of things. Everyone made their assumptions of me. As I worked hard to make things easier for them, they only saw one side. This happens all too often.

Last week when I had called my bonus mom, because she is exactly what I need when I need it. When I am at a spiritual block, when I need to understand her son, when I need to be picked up. That morning I talked to her, God took me to a place in the Bible saying, "Just see with your eyes and hear with your ears and ask God to show you all you need to see." When I told her all about my stressful work situation, she said the same exact thing. She then gave me instruction to declare God brings peace to my building every morning, and for God to bind the hands of the enemy there.

That morning I did just that and had the strength to go in and immediately change the vibe. Just as busy, but I was able to answer questions very calmly and lighten the atmosphere again.

My strength had been going down. I was getting discouraged, I was more stressed, and when I stopped reading and talking to God through it all, I started falling. When I came back to God, things started falling back in place. Suddenly we were laughing again, we were getting things done, and we had potential employees lined up, coming to the door for a job every day. Things were mending. Please, God, help me stay on this course. I want to be a good mom to all of our kids and enjoy this journey with my husband as we go through what I hope to be a magical experience in having our first child together one day.

During all my uncertainties, especially about COVID-19, God took me to Mark 1:29–34 where Jesus took the fever out of a woman and said, "Do not be scared." He told me to go to page 39 in the book I was reading, and it talked about having eyes to see and ears to hear. I did ask to hear with my ears and see with my eyes, God. I'm not hearing You. What did I miss?

Talk to Me, Lord

August 29, 2020

The last few weeks, I have come out to the porch and encountered wasps, digger bugs, new to me from Ohio. They are crazier than wasps, and every time, I'll go in the house or start swatting like a mad lady. But today I had a butterfly on the screen that looked like it couldn't move. I just knew it couldn't fly because I stared at it so long and took a picture. When I tried to help it, he flew away but came back. I thought of how I didn't instantly want to kill the butterfly. It didn't want to get away from me too fast. The wasps were crazy and trying to get away from me faster than me with them. It made me then think to racism. These wasps can hurt us. We have a history of it. What if they have a history of us swatting at them and can't wait to get away from us from a history of fear?

The butterfly was chill because we don't have a violent history together. When you are always keeping one eye open for the wasp to strike, it will. Do we hate a breed of dog so bad, we'd hurt it if it came near us? Sadly some can say yes, and maybe they do. That is hate. That is not the love of God. Would you belittle, hurt, or even condone the killing of someone because they love a person of the same sex? Sadly again, some say yes. Sadly most of those claim to be religious. If it is you reading even this book right now, if you know even a few words in the Bible you know that it claims we are to love all, God does not say yes, that person is wrong or their behavior is wrong, so go ahead and judge them for me. Go ahead, and hate them.

When the gate opens, all of His sheep will know His voice and follow. I need to know that voice. I have to hear it. No matter how great your ears are, you can't hear what isn't being said for you. How many things can you think of that you may have thought or done to keep from hearing that voice? At the time, you may not even know you did anything wrong until your emotion took over and you thought about it after. Or if you stay so busy, you don't ever stop and think about it and may never know.

I have wanted to know God for a while now. I went to church way more as a young mother than I do now or did until recently, but I had no idea there was more to it than just sitting there on Sunday. Why won't this work for me? Of course, I am broken. I go every week, I have genuine care and concern for others, and my character won't let me do anyone any intentional wrong or harm. I feel horrible if I accidentally do. Why can't I hear Him?

Childhood wasn't amazing for my sister and me, to say the very least as I mentioned. One day I got to see my sister be a mother, and she was doing it just like I did when my kids were little. Like every day is going to be magical for my kids no matter what. They will want to love their life, and we went (and one still going) to the extreme. All that pressure for our kids to just not say their childhood sucked. That's not enough. We wanted (want, LOL) them to think back to their childhood and miss it so much. Partially because we were (are) having another childhood too.

Took me a while to understand that's why it actually was so fun for the kids, because I was thoroughly enjoying myself too. But I stayed so busy trying to achieve this, I never realized I didn't ever slow down enough to see life. I took it very extremely. My house always had to be perfect, smell perfect, have perfect food served there at any time. And I had to be perfect too.

When it all broke my back and I just wanted to be me again, I found out my boys loved to just go to lunch with me, talk, sit on the porch, joke, or laugh at the dining room table. Every weekend didn't have to be fireworks and ten-mile bike rides. In fact, they later joked about how I wore them out and was crazy and dangerous or just tough. What mom gets up on her day off, works out for an hour, mows the grass, and then takes her kids on a long bike ride in the heat of August, then makes a huge dinner, cleans up, and never stops moving, creating, sewing, painting, volunteering, working, cleaning? I'm tired just remembering it. I moved so fast that it was aggravating when almost anyone wanted to have a conversation with me. And I certainly didn't sit down and relax and talk to God. Part of me was still thinking, "Yep, a voice is going to suddenly come from the sky." Wanting it, but not really believing it, not even understanding it.

I am taken to Luke 10:25–37.

In this story, the lawyer continues to want more detail of what neighbor actually means? He can't seem to understand or accept that it means anyone he comes in contact with. He continues to ask questions, hoping God has blocked certain people from the category of neighbor. People he doesn't feel like he should have to love. Them people that aren't neighbors. Sound familiar?

Jesus's story put him in his place with the parable, saying, "Does it matter who he is or what the person was who passed him?" Not at all. Show mercy now. There is no room for your own interpretation of what that means. Can you explain when your life is over that it was okay to not help someone in that state or condition because they were gay? Or a different color?

Will he say, "Oh, okay, I completely understand why you didn't want to help them then, or even treat them as I would"? If that's what you think, that's what you have convinced yourself because you stay too busy to have real thoughts. Continuing on, I am taken to Martha and Mary in Luke 10:38–42: "As Jesus and His disciples were on their way, He came to a village where a woman named Martha opened her home to Him. She had a sister called Mary, who sat at the Lord's feet listening to what he said. But Martha was distracted by all the preparations that had to be made. She came to Him and asked, 'Lord, don't you care that my sister has left me to do the work by myself? Tell her to help me!' 'Martha, Martha,' the Lord answered, 'you are worried and upset about many things, but few things are needed—or indeed only one. Mary has chosen what is better, and it will not be taken away from her.'" If you don't slow down to listen, how can you be mad you can't hear? Once I physically could not read anymore. My eyes continued to push moving forward, but the words became jumbled and took me back to my conclusion, which was if one can gain entrance into heaven and eternal life, nothing else matters. To those who complain, we can only point out that the choice is ours (*Son of God and You*, page 139). I knew I was finished for today.

CHAPTER 9

When People Get in the Way

September 5, 2020

Interestingly enough, I continue in my book to read about the laborers who all were paid the same at the end of the day despite the fact that some started early, worked twelve hours in the sun, and some were hired in the last hour of the day when there was no sun. I couldn't understand His parable (Jesus) that the last will be first, and the first will be last. The people that were there first grew angry about the fact that they were paid the same as those who worked an hour with no sun. Most were angry and resentful instead of grateful He had kept His promise to them (Matthew 20:1–16).

As a manager, I know this parable in real life. Your constant mission is try to make things better and take care of everyone, but typically, not all, but many are only on your side when it is good for them. The minute they are unhappy about anything, you are immediately the bad guy. No one cares about what you do behind the scenes. Or what others do behind the scenes negatively, or even what they themselves do behind the scenes to negatively impact you, others, or the business. God speaks that this is the same for entering heaven. If you are hateful toward someone who has done a lot of wrong because one day after all of their wrong they choose to change and to love Jesus and God and get into heaven, hopefully with you, but are you going to enter if you let your heart fill up with anger or resentment for them coming in late or for anything for that matter?

If someone is not my religion, am I going to get angry and fight with them on why I know more about God than them so God will let me into heaven for defending Him and hating this person? Does that really sound right? If we really have only two places we can go (which we do), and we can get it together now, no matter what we've done, why wouldn't we? Because most think they can always jump on board later and do whatever they want today. Or ask for forgiveness Sunday and do it all over again. What if Judgment Day came on a Wednesday? Or you know He has to come on a Monday when we are hating the alarm clock after the weekend. Or cursing about who at work might tick us off on the first day back today. Or how we want to throw in the towel and quit. Maybe become a cashier so we can just scan things. Or a greeter to only have to say hello. Not thinking about the challenges those positions may experience also. Those people who think there's always tomorrow will probably ruin those positions also. They ruin them all because they don't think they have to treat others a certain kind of way today. This in turn is what puts the world on edge.

There are people all around that think there's always tomorrow or think they don't have to believe, that they are only going in the ground when life is over. And there are those who see beauty in the world. Those that even though there are "everlasting tomorrow people" everywhere, they are still beautiful because God made them for a reason. He made them to be the last ones paid who make just as much in order to see how His twelve-hour workers will respond to them. This life is a constant test.

So will you cuss about them in your head in the morning. How will you hate the person who is always asking dumb questions or slowing everyone down, the one who never seems to do enough or have to help, the ones who are asking you to do better all the time, or the ones who simply won't do better? Instead, YOU will have to change. You have to slow down, listen to those questions you may initially think are stupid, and instead see the opportunity to teach them, because they felt safe enough to ask you in the first place. What will happen when you've answered all of their questions? I realized in leadership that no one thinks exactly the same. Not even close.

Each department thinks a similar way but all different at the same time, a different perspective, or areas of importance and focus, different struggles or challenges. In order to get them all to relate to each other is a struggle every single day, because the opportunity to misunderstand each other is lurking around every corner for failure. And this is the same in life. Different groups of people who know the history and experiences of their lives offend each other without trying. If the other side is looking and listening for it, which unfortunately happens all the time, if they are listening and asking questions to understand that other person's upbringing or experiences, they could probably understand their beliefs. It does not make them wrong. It makes you so fortunate to believe in something you know to be true. If you really feel that strongly, you must have seen or heard something to guide those thoughts or you are pushing off tomorrow's.

Most people know the verse about if a man doesn't work, he doesn't eat. But what I learned next spoke to me louder than that. Who has shall be given. Those that don't shall have taken what little they do have, and as someone who has had very little all of my life, that didn't make sense. I struggled financially up to exactly 32 until things got easier and easier. When I thought about it again now at 35 with no major financial struggles and thought about the moment it turned around, I realized people with everlasting tomorrows had caused that too. In the beginning, people who didn't work and wanted everyone to bend over backward to help pay their bills, being my mother. Who knows what all made her this way? There were 2.5 billion reasons of hers to choose from. From that to someone else who ended up exactly the same way, and I was the expected one to foot the bill, being my ex-husband. These people were always going to live their lives differently tomorrow.

They took everyone for granted and only needed you if you helped them. When I left the torment of what they both caused me, I was free. No longer bogged down with all the negativity they brought including financially, life became comfortable. I could have not been struggling for about the last ten years beforehand at least on my own and could have before that if I had to. I literally started to receive good news after good news after I freed myself. Blessings came every couple of months, and now I sit here on this beautiful porch with the sun beaming lightly on my face near the pond, listening to the nature all around, birds, frogs, and wind on the trees, talking with God about how I did this past week along this journey, what I could have done differently, what I should do again, and what I need to do in order to continue getting better, to being taught more about faith and what it can do for you. To taking a trip to reflect and watch how it did, and immediately pray and discuss how I want it to continue. Knowing my strengths, what makes me truly happy and pleasing God, to share all He is giving me to someone else's needs by doing it, that's always when I was reinforced to write more. What makes me happy is de-stressing on this porch, hearing these amazing sounds, and expanding my mind, all while figuring out the secrets of life and how to be truly happy and peaceful from the source Himself. When I listen, when I let Him.

Even the possibility of sharing that with others is such an amazing feeling. That would be one more gift I could reflect back on that He has given me. Having these thoughts and growing on them is enough to reflect on and be thankful. This doesn't come to just your mind. We have all been given a mental capacity of some sort. Some more than others. But we all have a spirit inside us that is connected with THE spirit. When that happens, you don't need to be smart. All you need to know on what to say and do will be provided to you right when you need it. If you asked for it, if you listen for it. If you let Him. It is just as amazing as it sounds, and I wish I would have learned this much earlier in my life. However, I am so thankful to have learned it at all. There are so many that never will.

I have money for a massage today to release stress, children happy in the distance, and I can't wait to see, hug, kiss, smell, love my husband when he comes home. Because he is my best friend and partner in life, he was one of those blessings that came every other month before I even knew how to pray. I had love in my heart and always had been humble and kind naturally, so much so that almost everyone aimed to break that, and to some degree they did, until I was broke. I had been seeking God all my life, but I had no idea all I needed to do was to go to Him. People who truly believed always seemed to have it together, were never worried, it seemed. How do I get that? Help me.

Thinking I had to be perfect to get that, along with all the things I had been through, eventually made me cold. Why am I always holding the world together? And He doesn't even talk to me. But when it was all just too much and too exhausting to pretend I was holding it together, I let go of the fact I couldn't do it alone, He then stepped in and caught me. I went through so much at once, even later in life. Freedom, uncertainty right after from losing my job, happiness of a new beautiful relationship, and fear of if I would be okay financially, and would losing my job put too much stress on my new relationship that I had just been convinced would last forever.

Would I once again be doing things on my own, or should I believe that this man that I tore down my walls for will be here through it all and support me as a team? I hadn't seen that one before, so I was definitely skeptical.

Each time something that could have broken me came my way, it was turned into something else that led to a great path. I think of today's challenges and how they are harder than ever in this world, in this political season, and racism and hate present in the world, at work with way more challenges than I have ever had, needing strong actions to move forward positively, and being comforted to know next week He will guide me. Each Saturday, I will learn what I need to do better, and I am excited to see what I can say next year this time on what came out of it, and what my life looks like now because He has the wheel. I want to let Him, no matter who tries to get in the way.

CHAPTER 10

When God Works through People for Your Good

September 12, 2020

Matthew 25:14–30 seems to be a parable about how we must use the gifts God has given us, and live the way it is instructed in the Bible, or we might just be forgotten altogether on Judgment Day. If you believe, that causes a little stress and a quest for more answers. Or if you know your gift and the way your lifestyle should be, but don't think you can conform to some of the stuff that seems to be expected of you, I'm sure you're not alone. I really thought that too. Maybe like me, you thought I don't seem to have any gifts, and I don't hear what God is supposed to be telling me. I seem to be punished all the time, but I would never truly hurt someone and know what's right and wrong in my heart. I never curse God. I just thought I wasn't special enough! I also couldn't understand why I seemed to be challenged, stressed, forced to be a tense, cold, hard person from my surroundings nonstop.

It makes it even harder to keep trying for that relationship when life seems to be punching you all over repeatedly without a break! I've definitely been there since a very young age. It just seemed like everything I went through was a joke. The older I got, the longer the story got, and I just made jokes of all the things that stacked up against me. Having daddy issues, as they say, for not having a dad or any of his family. My mother, I don't need to say any more. The molestation at five that the devil still sometimes tells me was my own fault. The abuse of a stepfather with anger issues. Living in an unstable home where water or lights could be shut off at any time, where six months was a long time to live somewhere, to only having eight years of school out of twelve, to being very educationally behind, and the whirlwind of my adulthood were even scarier.

Fighting back, I got my GED when I was nineteen or twenty and fought so hard at work to overcome my lack of education. I made it into management and decided to go to college online. Struggle consumed my life with also having two small children, a full-time career, and a spouse that was more harm than good. They promoted me right before I graduated, and I went to Washington, DC, to finally walk the stage for a diploma after so much hard work, sacrifice, and dedication. Something I was actually excited for and never thought I would ever get to do. Once I exited the stage and saw everyone being embraced and celebrated by their loved ones, I was met with a stuffed animal aggressively shoved in my stomach that took my breath away afterward, followed by "let's go." I thought all my hard work had paid off after only have being an operations manager about a year if that they were asking me to go to North Carolina to open up a building.

I had been telling everyone at work since day one when I first started as a part-time associate that I wanted to go to the Carolinas for some reason. The Carolinas had called me back ever since the first time I drove through it. I never really thought it would happen. Now with the opportunity in front of me, I still felt like it was where I needed to be without question. I had to convince others this was where we needed to go, and get two kids excited about leaving everyone we knew. It was very scary at times, dealing with the finances and putting your kids in a good area, schools, safety, etc. But it was like all my steps were guided. I wasn't actually scared. I was afraid of what could happen along the way, but for some reason, I knew it was the right decision. My career was going great as I got to use my knowledge to assist with the setup of a building from scratch. It was exciting. I clicked well with everyone in my office, it seemed, and with the way we all worked together, things seemed to be going positively. However, at home, I was a stressful mess. When I got tired of being afraid, choked, kicked, shoved, and with the severity growing all too quickly, after the worst night ever, and with the help, love, support from a wonderful friend, I was able to be freed. A friend that I knew in Ohio from my job had went from Ohio to Wisconsin and then wanted to apply where I was in North Carolina. It ended up working out that he was hired, and his family relocated at the same time I did. Without any friends anywhere, it was nice to know someone, but their house was very different than mine. Love of God and each other was very present. Without them and encouragement from his wife, I would maybe be dead. Oddly enough, right before I was left alone, just like that, they had accepted another transfer.

But they were there for me exactly when I needed them. Like they had been placed there for exactly one year to push me and help me through a horrible life-changing situation. That's what God does without you knowing. I know now I should have been praying through it all, asking for what I needed. But my friends were doing it for me without me even knowing.

Shortly after I was freed and began living again, hanging out with great friends from work, helping me through it all, a partnership at work that had been easy since day one suddenly started growing in a different direction. We both had been through very difficult and hurtful marriages. We were both separated and anticipating full freedom. We were both having a great time. We didn't have family close, and so a few of us had become family. When it was evident my work partner was perfect for me to me and everyone else, I slowly tried to take my guard down, some days still trying. I was so scared of being controlled and hurt physically and mentally again. I was okay with our relationship one day, and then an independent woman who didn't want or need him or anyone for that matter the next day. Every ledge he talked me off, patiently and lovingly, made me feel stronger about him. He once compared me to the ocean, pulling him in with the current and then pushing him out with the next wave.

All my male stereotypes that had entered in my head from what I had seen so far in life were challenged and shockingly did not apply to him. It's very difficult to reprogram your head, I have learned. The devil would tell me bad things about him, trying to control me, and after we talked about it, it didn't make any sense at all. My now husband took the time to heal me and love me through all of those thoughts. Sometimes I'm not sure how, because I would be very convinced. I was taught through him and my wonderful bonus momma that talking to God is what helps identify and stops those thoughts. Many conversations with both of them through tears turned me around again. Sometimes I didn't believe what they said. I really wanted to. I remember a conversation with my bonus momma when work was caving in on me. Anything bad that could've happened was, and it was beyond stressful. After listening to me rant through tears for about an hour, offering questions along the way at the end, she would say, "I don't know the exact answers, but I know THE answer. Every morning, you're going to walk through the door and say, 'God, declare peace in this building for all that enter through, bind the hands of the enemy in this place,' and, honey, you've got to mean it."

I prayed it every morning that week and the next and the next. And people came to the door for jobs, as staffing was my largest concern. The first day, I had to really try and say it like she did, but by the end of the week, it was flying off my tongue as I watched the train get back on the tracks. This wasn't the first time this had happened, but every time I stepped away from prayer, something else bad began to happen. The first time I experienced this for sure was when I lost my job, and my beautiful auntie, sister to my bonus momma, met me for lunch with a spiritual book called *The Power of a Praying Woman*. I'd never really read the Bible because it confused me, but that book started to explain to me what I had been missing.

CHAPTER 11

He Will Guide You

September 19, 2020

Your entire life will be guided. That was the first thing that I was compelled to write. It's one of those rare mornings I love when I will pop my eyes open at 5:00 a.m., wait for my love to kiss me goodbye for work, get up, and start this time with God. It has been such a stress reliever to sit on this porch, coffee, hot pack around my neck, and a blanket. I relax until I feel compelled to grab the pen and am told what to say at exactly the right moment. Most of the time, I don't even read the previous page or chapter to refresh myself for it to make sense, but it doesn't matter because it's not a story. It's being told to me, the more time I have and the more tranquil the atmosphere, like no one else is up, no noise from neighbors, cars, or anything, just nature turned all the way up. The more time in that atmosphere I spend and open up my mind for God, the more He shares with me.

The problem comes in when everyone's problem is solved. This was not my thought today; it was pressed hard into my mind. I thought of those that just don't believe at all. Those that secretly doubt, those that question themselves. They don't want to believe God doesn't exist really, but seriously wondering if they're losing their minds. I was the one wondering if I was losing my mind for several reasons, mainly for the life I had lived so far. When I explained my childhood to anyone up to my life just a few years ago, I would secretly sit back and wonder how the hell I was still good inside. All these people and things that should have destroyed me, how am I still sane, not in prison, or hiding in my house?

But still I am trying to be a positive influence for people that have went through the same things. I've been told I'm annoying for this reason, but I couldn't figure out how so many people took the other road instead. It doesn't seem appealing to me at all. The number of people I have told even one of my stories to was to console or encourage someone who had told me about their story that was similar to just one of mine. They are everywhere. And most of the time, I have a story for each of theirs. I think to myself I am annoying to try and help you to look up and not spend an eternity as a bitter, pissed-off, miserable person, and possibly if they don't turn back to the narrow road in hell with gnashing teeth. People who don't read the Bible or go to church may not know exactly that there are gnashing teeth (I didn't), but those who never read the Bible and have very little knowledge of faith still know hell is supposed to be really bad. So all should think about it even if there is a possibility.

If your life is totally guided. After my thoughts rambled on about thoughts and more thoughts, it is guided again and again. After my eyes pop up wide open on a Saturday morning after my workweek, to your life is guided write it down now, then I feel pulled to read whichever spiritual book I'm in the middle of right now, right here. When I do, I am immediately led to talks about how the decision had been made for the death of Jesus. He just kept moving on, healing people, teaching them, and not caring at any time someone could kill Him or capture Him. On top of that, He is sometimes going toward those miserable people who seem like the most dangerous, yet every time, He had no fear and was always successful either to heal with words or touch. These behaviors should have completely confirmed any doubts about who He was, but now they are going to kill Him for it.

His life was guided, and He fully knew it. So is ours. What happens when you get what you prayed for? Life is good or better, and you may feel that you don't really need to pray anymore. After time goes by that may be a very long span, or it could be about a month, you have a reason to come back to prayer. After you are let down so it seems so many times, you may come to the conclusion there is no one up in the sky that is going to tell me it will be okay one more time. I'm not going to coach my brain into that ever again. Even I don't believe myself anymore. Some go all the way and can say it out loud to others freely, and some are ashamed that they even say it in their own head, but they do. Again, I was the latter of the two. Why do I feel so bad, and why am I even thinking there can't be someone looking out for me, or if there is, he definitely needs to be fired. Maybe your prayer stops altogether, or you do it but don't believe what you're praying for could happen. You are officially on the wide-open path the majority of the world's population is going on just like that.

One of the most powerful things I had read in my journey to understand was Matthew 7:13–14: "Enter through the narrow gate, for wide is the gate that leads to destruction and many enter through it. But small is the gate and narrow the road that leads to life and only a few find it." It was powerful to me because I had seen so many people going through the big gate, and they didn't even seem to care. But my next thought was if only a few find the straight and narrow, will they live in eternity? Even as I write this, I know I've had thoughts I would not feel comfortable saying to God on Judgment Day, but they just happen before I even knew it. I always felt bad after, but am I doomed for the possibility of gnashing teeth because of those thoughts or actions? I always ended up cussing by the end of the week. My neck was always tight. I made fun of someone at work who was stressing me out for whatever the reason was. I let the enemy tell me a few times I was hideous, that no one is loyal, so why do you even try to connect to people, build them up, or try to make them feel good too, or try to just be upbeat, hoping it will be contagious? Just stop caring, and do what's fun for you. I never have left that voice go on too long before I came back. I hadn't even realized I was going down the wide road again. The time that lapsed in the beginning seems long, so you're okay when you have to come back to prayer the second time. Okay, I may have gotten out of control.

Maybe yelling at the guy who passed me and honked the horn, or the ones we see more than family are wearing us down and we can't do a thing about it, or snapping at my family because of my fifty-plus-hour workweek. Early on, I guess it could've been I drank too much. I talked too much about other people and didn't value feelings as much as I should have. Whatever the reason, hey, God, I'm back. I need help again. You are under the impression when things get even slightly better, it's already time to say, "Thanks, God, but I'm good now, and I'll see You next time." You may even read or go to church a couple of times in between, singing loudly and dancing like you came up with a church routine. But your next reason to come back will be coming sooner each and every time to begin to let you know you don't know better than He does. The cycle begins again, and each time, that doubt you may even feel bad about gets stronger. Like I was told the problem comes after you get what you prayed for. I'll admit when things are good, I wasn't praying as hard. But what should happen is your relationship changes with God when you consistently work on it. Instead of praying for what you need only when you need it, you could be praying for guidance on what you want, you could be asking for guidance on what you've done wrong, and then acknowledge it was wrong, listen to how to fix it, then do that. We give up because we assume it's not working, but it's our Father saying, "Pay attention and learn, or I will make you." Most don't understand that, and after so much disappointment, they completely give up on what they believe to be a failing relationship with God that's not really possible in the first place. No one told me I didn't have to be perfect, or I would have been here a long time ago.

In fact, it always sounded exhausting to be a child of God. I can't even have wine again? Didn't His Son make water wine? Seems a little unfair. No one told me I could still be myself and have fun too. Or that God has given you so many ways to enjoy life and wants you to. Just not at the expense of hurting others, yourself, or walking with the enemy. When you walk back into your small slightly better problem taken care of with a week or two or four of praying, just know it isn't cured. We think, say, or do things we may or may not even realize every single week that are not good. How do you learn about them to get better at handling them? Small problems uncured turn into bigger ones. What if what you prayed for didn't cure you as much as you would think? Maybe you left the guided tour. I was taken to a place in my book that talks about how Jesus was telling His disciples how easy it is to get all that you want. By the sound of it, who could believe that? Starting at Matthew 21:18, Jesus tells a fig tree it will never produce fruit again and it withers up and dies. The disciples are amazed it withered up right away, and asked Jesus how He did it. Jesus said it like this (verse 21): "Truly I tell you have faith and do not doubt, not only can you do what was done to the fig tree but you can say this to a mountain go throw yourself into the sea and it will be done. If you believe you will receive what you ask for in prayer."

If you let Him, but you must BELIEVE Him.

To Let Him, You Must Believe Him

September 26. 2020

Thankfully, it's another one of those mornings. The thought that pops me up today as I got snapped into feeling the earth move for just a few split seconds and then back to reality was we can't see the earth moving, can we? But it is. Two weekends in a row, I woke up at 4:30 a.m., listened to my husband get ready for work while lying in bed because I can't go back to sleep. I kiss him goodbye, go back outside to this routine, and why am I so excited about it? I'm dragging myself out of the bed at the last minute by Friday for work, but here I am excited to be up at 4:30 a.m. on a Saturday morning. I once thought it was absolutely more than enough to show up at church a few times a year, and here I am excited more and more when I get close to Saturday waking up at 4:00 a.m., spending three hours talking to God, and wondering where I can find time to do it more. It was so hard to get into this routine. Now I don't want to miss an opportunity. The more I listen, the more I hear. Suddenly every Christian song begins to make sense now and sometimes country songs too. My choice of music has even changed. But suddenly you start to see who has a serious relationship with God and who just goes to church a few times a year on Sundays. Who may be struggling themselves to be good, needing to go back every Saturday for forgiveness and questions. I had definitely found myself there. My old ways and thoughts creeping in by Friday when I had had enough with everything around me. I needed Saturday morning to be shown the things I was too stupid to see during the week. I would feel a change at work with the energy now and then, and every time, it pointed back to when I had to focus on one aspect of the business harder than another, the other side began to fall apart. I couldn't prove they did anything specifically. They all just began to lose control. I had this happen several times. Something else needed my attention, and the left side seemed to be doing something every time I turn my back that's devastating to the business, but how was I going to get it back on track without losing sight of the right side too? This is what I'm worrying about when suddenly my eyes seem to go crossed, and I am seeing and feeling the earth move. I quickly snapped back to reality and tried my hardest to see it again. I even asked God to show me again, but instead in my mind, I hear the earth moves, but you can't see it. You can never really slow down enough to notice. You can find out where things go wrong without all the details. How? By pinpointing the shift and you'll know why. Faith can't be borrowed. Faith can't be faked. Faith can't be used or turned on like a light when the room gets dark. If it is a true relationship, you have true faith, and before the light goes just a little dim, you are shown how to make it bright again. You are never left alone in the darkness. When you stay lost in the darkness, never asking for a match back to the light switch, you leave much room for evil to slip in and live in darkness permanently.

I once asked if I would know His voice when I hear it, what if I just don't hear it. But I have read many verses where Jesus refers to His people as "those He has chosen," so even though we may not hear what He is saying yet, the more you are following Him, you know what He asks of you. You will be blessed.

October 10, 2020

You will have eyes to see and ears to hear when you come in. The experience I had probably would've scared me before all the recent experiences I had been having. Upset with myself for sleeping in this morning until 8:30 a.m. Not wanting to short myself of the time for my weekly experience, I lay back and felt the earth move again, but this time, I didn't have to only see it for two seconds. I could look around. The thought came to my mind of which way the earth was moving. I just knew it. I sat and watched the direction it was clearly going. And then it stopped, and was moving a different direction. I could've sworn it was moving forward, and when I fully believed that, it moved to the left. Every time I tried to reassure myself it was going forward, it would stop completely when I doubted it. I would see it again, and again after much focus, it was going to the left. The thought of eyes to see and ears to hear. If you believe Him for everything, He will show you. Think of how many bad decisions you could avoid by listening to Him tell you the right ones to make. Only problem is you have to truly want to do the right things and truly believe God is in control of your life. I tried to think of what could happen if I had eyes to see and ears to hear. My bonus momma and my husband tell me that all the time. I once told my bonus mom I read where God said, "I send you out as a sheep amongst wolves." I told her I only see sheep until the wolf bites me, from always wanting to see or look for the good in others. I told her that she and her son could see every wolf from miles away, and they can. These people are His people. Normal people making mistakes, asking for true forgiveness and guidance, truly loving people. I was so nervous to meet my black mother-in-law when my husband and I started dating. The first time I met her, we surprised her; we had only talked on the phone once before real quick. All her sisters knew we were coming for her birthday dinner with them, and once one of her sisters came and got us and took us to her, I was so nervous. Will they be okay with me? I'm white, I'm a Midwestern girl, so that's the North according to the South, but basically, I'm different. She instantly made that all go away the way she hugged me and shouted when she saw me.

The same with her sisters. And we had genuine conversation where I knew they not only accepted me for me, but also they were excited about us and our relationship. Because they have eyes to see, they saw that I was a sheep, not a wolf, regardless of the differences. But they probably saw that at the time I was a lost one. I was also scared that I wasn't gifted or special enough to be in their family. I honestly didn't know much about the Bible other than the main points, and if they had asked me to say a prayer before eating, they would have enjoyed my family chant from when my cousins were in Lutheran preschool thanking Jesus for this meal repeatedly like a nursery rhyme. Even if they knew this from sight, they never let me know it. When I lost my job and my husband's aunt had lunch with me and she was still so excited about my life, I tried to be. But the first time in my life since the age of fifteen, I didn't have a job all of a sudden. After twelve years of hard work and working my way up the ladder, then opening a building successfully, I was no longer needed. She wasn't scared at all. She gave me this notebook I'm now writing in, and a book called *The Power of a Praying Woman*. After I was displaced from work, I went and bought my woman's Bible, but I couldn't stay focused on reading it. Then I started reading the book she gave me and the Bible verses where it said to, and I instantly began to learn a little. My life started repairing itself quickly. Nervously I declined the first position offered to me where I had interviewed three hours away on the beach because I was frantic and didn't want to let an opportunity go by and end up with nothing. My now husband drove me three hours away for this interview, telling me how I would do awesome and there was no need to worry. We had great conversation outside of reminding me of my current situation. My first time interviewing outside of the company I had been with since age twenty-one, and for a management position, which I had earned those there in the past more so than interviewed for them. I did so good in the interview and had all the five guys interested in my answers and laughing at the humor I threw out every now and then too. I knew I had the job when I left. I was so happy with myself, and so was my husband when I told him, but then we both got very quiet after discussing what would happen when they called me back. Would I drive three hours one way, would me and the boys move there until my future husband found a place to transfer, and would our new relationship that was amazingly strong already be able to handle this? When that call came, we took a chance on declining it so that we wouldn't have to be without each other. We all prayed to God. We prayed alone and together. My bonus momma prayed over me on the phone and had her pastor's wife pray for me over the phone. They prayed so passionately like they had no doubt God would step in, none. And I got a call from the same company that offered me the first position three hours away, asking me to come to their Greensboro branch and interview there. They weren't upset with me for declining but wanted me somewhere else. And just like that, I never missed a paycheck. This is what praying for others and ourselves can do, and meaning it. I didn't have the same confidence that God was going to answer me, but they did. And that's why they see.

I mean no harm to my family by saying I didn't know much about God. We all need to have a teacher. Someone to guide you there, and many to continue guiding you on the way. My family believed in God. We prayed for food when we were all together. We went to church sometimes. But no one seemed to truly have a relationship with God. But we didn't know how or that you really needed to. We would say God will make everything okay, but only wanted to believe it because we hadn't really seen it. Our mother many times made us pray for things I felt bad about praying for. "Let's pray for winning the lottery because I spent the money my grandmother gave me to pay the rent." Why would God let that happen for you? You asked for a blessing because you spent all of your own money, or really the money your husband had earned, then pushed your elderly grandmother into being nice enough to give it to you, but then you spent that too. Why would you be blessed with more free money you didn't earn? Of course, it didn't happen, but out of nowhere, someone else would help her. Sometimes a little, but sometimes a lot. I believe those were the small answers to our prayers as kids, praying we get just a small break here and there from the repetitive letdowns and worries about our own fate. I'm not sure we knew how to pray or whom to pray to. We just wanted to be freed from this continuous turmoil. If you've watched *Bruce Almighty*, you clearly see why God doesn't give everyone what they prayed for. You can't pray for something that is evil. Your husband beats you. You can't wish for him to get beat up and learn a lesson, or worse. I know. It doesn't change anything. But when the prayer turns into "Lord, I am so lost, so weak and tired, I haven't been able to handle this on my own. Please just guide me out no matter how," He will if you let Him, but only if you believe that He can and will.

Giving me a deep desire to move six and a half hours away, happening to be near a good friend that helped me through and be right with me when I needed them to be for the next good chapter of my life without even knowing the path, that was God. I had no idea, but at the same time, my future husband was moving to the same area, and was praying for me. You can't go back to praying for things of immaturity when you see the large impacts God can make on your life when you give Him the freedom to do so. For a long time, I had prayed for a man that would make me feel so safe and loved and cared for. One that was helpful with our life financially and physically and worked as one, as a team for our life. After not receiving any of these things for so long, I gave up completely. I wanted nothing to do with a relationship. I later married a man that moved to the same area I did for the exact same reasons of giving up on truly feeling loved. We once high-fived as work partners that we would never get married again. I have two boys, and he, two girls. At the time seven, eight, nine, and eleven, I think. Now they are twelve, twelve, fourteen, and sixteen. Both oldest's names start with a D, and both youngest's with a K. They came together for the first time, and we instantly felt like family. My husband was the male support the boys always needed and eventually the discipline too. And I had two little girls hugging and kissing me, wanting to do my hair and have me do theirs too. That wanted to be around me all the time, and loved all my clothes, and noticed things the boys naturally just didn't. They were excited to cook with me and sing and dance in the kitchen. When they started calling me mommy, one much sooner than the other, which was a surprise to me both times, I had to hold back tears. I loved it so much and still do when we're all together.

And my heart feels like I'm giving my own children away every time they go home. I suddenly ask how I got here from where I had been, a loving husband, so much so that he completes me in every way, a beautiful family, and now family members I don't know how I ever lived without before.

There were many difficult situations in our first four years together. What has shocked me most is how my husband responds to those challenges. I am never a problem, and he will never treat me like one. We will talk, understand each other, and pray for each other. We will love each other and hurt for each other and pick each other up. That's what he has taught me, which is a wonderful change from keeping score, yelling, being hit or scared, or having to protect myself. Constantly feeling on edge, or that I am always a problem. How do you feel loved that way? The answer is always you can't. I have come so far and still have so far to go. My progress has only been made because when life got heavy and I tell these important people in my life they don't complain with me or discourage me, they pray without doubt.

CHAPTER 13

Being There for Others

October 11, 2020

"My people are destroyed through lack of knowledge" (Hosea 4:6).

What is the window or doorway you need to shut to accept the Lord into your life? It may be something you never knew of or expected. Lack of knowledge will keep us from the Lord.

A pastor that was new to ministry and also one of my employees came and talked with me on a Friday, just as I was about to leave for my weekend. Normally I would be pushing people out of my office at that point to start the relaxation and much-needed recovery! But I could tell this was going to be a conversation I needed to have. I thought I needed to listen. He had also taken the time to get a card for me since it was Bosses Day, which is always great to get positives rather than the usual problems and issues all day long. He gave me the card and said that he really appreciated me, along with some other positive compliments that were so nice to hear on this difficult work journey. *Maybe I have done a few things right*, I thought. But the motive really came out right after when he told me he was nervous about his first communion. He was looking for encouragement spiritually from me? Why? I kept thinking I don't know anything. I'm learning by myself right now. But I realized in the conversation we had what he was really beating himself up over, and I was able to lift him back up. He had been struggling on the job, and I would even be frustrated with the customers calling about his service opportunities, or the supervisor asking me what to do about him. But I would literally watch him, come into my office beaten down, and then literally watch him leave laughing and encouraged to keep trying and to keep moving forward.

Sometimes God was mentioned. But for the most part, it was just humble conversation about how I was so nervous with every new position I had that it had made me physically sick, and I made mistakes, but I got back up and moved on. That was enough to help someone else, and in turn, I always got lifted back up myself. Made me feel like this is who God's people are, and I also thought, *Oh my gosh, I am becoming one.* I can see the narrow road. It's faint and off in the distance, but I at least am on the right path. That day as we talked, he gave me two sentences of encouragement. He said, "It takes a partaker to be a peacemaker." It sounded promising, but I wondered what partaking really meant in this situation. The Google dictionary said, "To take part of something, to be involved with, to follow, to receive, or share." When I searched it in the Bible app, it says several verses. The one that caught my eye was 2 Timothy 2:6: "The husband man that laboureth must be first partaker of the fruits." So many things came to mind with this statement. You have to get involved (partake) to make peace. You have to work hard to earn that fruit though. The pastor of a friend's church I went to last Sunday, to be encouraging, said this that hit me, "It is so hard to be Christian," and it's true. You would never be able to be who we are supposed to be for God without repeatedly going back to be refilled with the joy and compassion that this world can beat out of you continuously.

Not everyone knows this, and so there are people who challenge your faith every day. But why? Because they are supposed to. Because when you learn that there is something else fighting to claim you, it will turn a light bulb on to you that all these challenges are a premade obstacle course just for you. God is like a parent trying to guide you through that course, and as all parents know, some don't make it to the other side. They get very distracted in the course and may stay a while or lose their direction altogether.

The second sentence was "A setback is a setup for a comeback." So many times in my life, something wonderful came out of something that I thought might break me. I would always look back and think first off how didn't it? Then second off, I'm so glad that I didn't break over that. I always used humor to laugh about the things that happened. It truly seemed to be funny until the story got longer and longer. I eventually only told pieces when asked, and then eventually it was harder to laugh. Everyone you come in contact with seems to have a motive, or not be who they said they would be. Very few people seem genuine, and even the genuine have issues. But that's why we have to be refilled with strength every day to keep going through the obstacle course without getting stopped or distracted on the way, trying to be good children to get on the narrow road. He said the other road is easy to find. It's so wide, many can go through so easily, like lost people that follow the flock before them. There are so many there because it's easy. But again being a Christian, loving all those people and everyone no matter what, is so hard.

I started reading again and was led to the part where Jesus was getting close to death. The world was caving in on Him. The more good He did, the more people thought He was crazy and wanted to shut Him up about His crazy God stuff. The saddest of all was even His own disciples turned on Him when they got caught with a group of nonbelievers and became one of them quickly to save His own life. Sound familiar? What was crazy to me was that Jesus knew before they deceived Him that they would. We are untrusting of people who haven't yet given us reasons to think they will deceive us. Jesus still let him be a disciple, loved him, taught him, and gave him blessings, knowing the whole time they would turn. Yet another reason to say loving like Jesus isn't possible? Or it seems impossible.

I am so passionate about how people should be with each other and so disgusted when people hurt each other and do such crazy things that I could never keep my mouth shut to my own detriment for so long. I've gotten better with age, but I think it's only because I don't do much else but go to work and home. I remove myself completely from other people's situations, only offering comfort if they need those words, but not offering to help them with the battle. The battles I felt I had to fight only caused more turmoil, more drama. Followed by none of those people you protected doing the same for you. If we could only all feel each other's pain, the world would be so peaceful. If everyone stopped fighting battles to change others' opinions, minds, or actions, just prayed for the peace that they needed and loved them through it, what on earth would that world look like? When we weren't living with or raising people harsh enough to bully someone, even someone with a disability that can't help it, or over the color of their skin they were born in that they can't help because they're different in some way, shape, or form, like we ourselves are the ideal of perfection, how conceited. Here's a very scary thought. Close your eyes and imagine you are that person dealing with your own hate and actions. How would life be, and how would you feel about the real you that you saw on the other side? If we could only feel each other's pain.

If God made seasons on the earth, named them seasons, and referred to new seasons, or going through this season of your life like it will eventually change, why worry if you don't like it now? The season will change.

Before Jesus was killed, He told Peter basically by the end of the night he would deny Him. Peter was adamant it would never happen. He saw all of Jesus's performed miracles and followed him and watched them. How could he deny Him? Peter followed Jesus to Annas, who assisted a high priest who wanted Jesus dead and to be silenced, but when they got there for Jesus's trial, Peter stayed outside, and when people outside asked him if he was a disciple, he said no. When they asked if he even knew Jesus, he said no. When they asked how they came together then, he said, "I have no idea what you're talking about." So do you know Him? If you get put under pressure by people who don't know Him, do you still? If you are being teased about the fact that you know Him, would you cave and say, "I have no idea what you talking about"?

Or would you make someone uncomfortable because they do know Him, because it just sounds too crazy to believe? Crazy as believing a demon of some sort entered someone you used to know but became someone else. Crazy as believing bad things may happen because of the bad things you may have done. We have all done bad things we're either aware of or not. But do you feel bad about them and ask for help to truly change, or do you feel bad but just say "oh well" and move on until the next time, or worse when you just don't feel bad anymore at all? You justify with yourself that others deserved what you gave them. But are we keeping score with the others' mistakes and downfalls, or are we loving and helping each other to the next season?

October 18, 2020

When you stop being so busy to mask your painful memories, you'll have to be ready to feel them. You may think that there is nothing residual there and be very shocked. I know I am. I work through with the help of my very patient and loving husband things I always thought would never bother me. Suck it up. I'm too strong to feel hurt. But peace is waiting on the other side to feel free and learn from those lessons, and you have them to teach others how to heal, and to show them it is possible. You know how and what to pray for because of them if you accept the Lord.

Sing Jubery, because He Knows More than We

October 31, 2020

My current lesson is separation anxiety is present in me and comes out often.

That was a thought that came to my head after my husband and I had a small disagreement. Because every time we do, I am immediately convinced he is leaving or unsatisfied, and my mind once again goes to flee mode, into "you don't need anyone" mode. "You've done this alone many times. Just think of 'us' (me)" mode. Of course, this is once again the enemy creeping in on my weaknesses, but it took me a long time to know, understand, and believe that, and then see the proof of knowing that. Thoughts that are negative, untrusting, and destructive come into our minds regularly. This is the battle. How we deal with it, that's what makes all the difference. Often when we go through things, we don't want to admit that they change us or take a toll on our minds and emotions. I definitely didn't. I was a strong, independent woman, and people that let things get them down are just weak. Once I had the time, knowledge, and support to understand that these issues show up in harmful ways in everyday life, I could definitely see them. Now in trying to accept and change the results, I am starting to be set free, obviously with the love and understanding of my creator.

Obviously, every time you disagree with your significant other, you shouldn't think they're leaving you, or that you should quit your job and run away and only think about yourself. This has happened to me for as long as I can remember. Convincing myself it is me against the world, and these thoughts were coming out even when my husband was having a bad week and just working through issues, which is something we all have to do from time to time. Once it was pointed out to me and I noticed where my head goes in these conversations, I was able to understand where it comes from. I spent a good part of my life trying to understand what I did wrong, or what was wrong with me for my father to walk away and never look back ever. For his whole family to know I existed but not care. Feeling isolated without my parents. My mother made me feel the same way as she was only concerned for herself, and very selfish. She made it seem with her words as though she lived for my sister and me, and we were her entire world, but the actions didn't line up with those words. She had a couple of boyfriends after divorcing my sister's father who tried to make me believe, and some did, that they were going to make up for my void by filling the open position. Of course, they all left, too, eventually. My sister's father left, too, and didn't even look back or have anything to do with her either. To me, this seemed normal. No one really stays forever.

The only regulars in my life were my grandparents whom I eventually moved in with as a teenager. Of course, he couldn't help it, but when the only faithful man that loved me passed away, that void grew deeper. He was the only rock in my life along with my grandmother. He was always whom I ran to for guidance and advice, and now that was gone too. Far too early. My first husband was also only concerned for himself, and I found myself alone in many situations where I should have been supported, including the birth of my first son. Because of selfish people, I had been left alone and put in many bad situations as a child, and now those situations put an instilled mentality in me that I didn't even recognize, that said no one will put me in a position to be hurt ever again. I don't need anyone; I will just leave before they do and not get hurt.

My husband recognized this early in our relationship. I will never forget how hard I cried when out of the blue, he said, "I'm not going anywhere, and I never want to hurt you, so you don't have to try to hurt me first." I was so shocked. I didn't even know that's what I was doing, but it made sense. I thought that people who talked about all the things they had been through were just trying to be the center of attention and get sympathy from others, and some do. But that was ethically not me. My one and only goal my entire life has been to laugh and enjoy life, to make others laugh and pick them up when they needed it. Seems like a very simple life goal, but grew harder each day, each month, each year. I often used my life experiences to make others laugh. But I never understood or wanted to admit that I needed to deal with them. My husband prays to God every day to be taught how to love me the way God wants him to love me and has since we've been together. I truly believe this is how he always knows what to say to me at the right moment, what I need when I'm feeling off, when something is wrong or different with me, and it's amazing. He hears these things from God much better than I do. My bonus mom has this gift also. I pray for hours to love my husband the way God wants me to also, but I don't hear as clearly as they do yet. But going from never hearing from the Lord to the experiences I've had recently and while writing this, I now know it's something I must work on continuously. I must continue to learn and seek God and have a relationship with Him, and the closer I get to Him, the more I will hear Him.

The way my husband is attentive to me is unbelievable. After my tubal reversal, I downloaded an app that recorded my cycles and told me the days I could get pregnant. Shortly after the surgery and healing, we went to Hilton Head to get away and spend a long weekend together. Because of the healing weeks and the way things lined up, I was convinced there was no way I could be pregnant yet. The thought had not yet even crossed my mind. The first day of our trip while we were getting ready to leave and go out, my husband told me I was already pregnant. I did not believe him, and when I asked to take a test, he said, "Let's just enjoy the weekend." I thought he was crazy. There were no signs, and I was to begin my cycle that Monday, and my body was telling me that was definitely going to happen. Until Monday came and it didn't. I took a test immediately after we got home, and in 2.5 seconds, that immediately confirmed what he somehow knew before I did.

November 14, 2020

God totally picked this house for me. Looking out of this beautiful scenery, He had to. When we were looking at houses, my husband was freaking me out, and probably the boys too. We like the country. We're from the Midwest and go home to ride four-wheelers for the weekend on someone's land we know. My husband had shown me beautiful houses, and I kept thinking it's just too much, too much house and too much money. Memories of losing houses as a kid kept flashing in my mind. I can't be that. I've been yelling at my mom for losing houses all my life. This one he scheduled us to see one night was my last hope after seeing a house in a development, yes, a country girl's worst nightmare, and then losing a beautifully decorated farm-style house to a higher bidder. I was distraught even though I knew our bid would have taken us to an uncomfortable number. It was a blessing my emotions didn't get us there. Thanks for the guidance, God! I knew if I kept doing that, I might get one as a lesson but suffer even more. So the house I'm optimistic about this particular night is country, but on a golf course and just large trees in between houses. A fancy undercover development. I was convinced I had to take this house because who knew what was next, and we had four kids piled up in basically a double wide home. It required us to go through a lot of prepping before the girls came, cleaning a boy's room to be acceptable, and having two boys bunk up together in each other's small bedroom. Then the girls never truly felt at home. So I love this house, I've convinced myself. My husband wants to slide in one more house at the last minute. Okay, let's get this over with. I'll admit while I was convincing him we had just left our new home. We popped around the corner, and I said, "Damn!" but more like "Daaaaaaaaaaammmmmmmmmmmmnnnnnnnnnnnn!" when we saw the house. Excuse my outburst of language! Too fancy on the outside, inside looks too bland. I have neighbors. There's no water around. Living room too small, master bath sucks. The list went on.

What I didn't see was an open canvas for us to paint and decorate like I love to and make it truly ours. Small living room with an open concept and tons of different places to sit for entertaining like I love to, a screened-in porch where I sit every Saturday because it takes my breath away, and many more hidden gems I couldn't see at the time, including this beautiful pond. It doesn't even have water near it. "Oh well, he says it's perfect for me, so let's do it." It wasn't until after we signed the papers when my husband told me he saw a big body of water close to our house on the property map. There was no way. I would have noticed that right away. We weren't supposed to go to the house until a certain date, but no one was living in it. I snuck over and walked to the edge of the property. When I looked all around frantically, I came to a place where the ground was getting softer and softer. I pushed through the trees in the brush, and there was this beautiful pond with an amazing view. Oh my God, I just bought this place! After we trimmed the trees a little bit, my future Saturday resting spot was created.

Everywhere I look it's beautiful, and I see the countertops that we made and designed that tell a story of how we did it, the funny things we said, experienced, and the fact that somehow, we didn't screw it up, but it's beautiful. The shiplap wall around the fireplace we all did up together, about twenty feet high, with us all afraid we would fall. We're so proud of these things, and we see our future version of it as we keep going. I learned God will always keep providing if I go to Him for direction and only truly believe. This view, God told me to take pictures of my exact moments. I called the experience today Jubery. I don't know what Jubery means, but the birds kept saying it back and forth in different pitches to each other, and it sounded beautiful. Like happiness. While birds splashed in the pond and frogs croaked. This is my house. That's what I say every weekend. My granddad always bought nice houses that he would fix up. Always had big dreams and made them happen. From pools to custom-painted designs by him, he never worried about losing his homes or not being able to pay his bills. My grandmother told me once he had lost his job and came home to deliver the news in a brand-new boat, saying it was no big deal. To his wife, that didn't work, and adding a new boat payment? He once told me to just let life happen. Always do your best and just don't be stupid, and God will take care of the rest. Oh, to be as light all the time as he was through anything. He lost his leg and drew smiley faces on "stumpy" to scare the grandkids with it. He was the only man in all our lives, and until my cousin Brandon and my own sons were born, he was surrounded by dramatic women. Stubborn, hardheaded women. He served our country in Vietnam twice and suffered horribly with Agent Orange. Yet he watched Disney movies every day and laughed his ass off. He made everyone laugh everywhere he went even when he was drowning in pain. My granddaddy was the only man that ever treated me right until my husband. From an absent father to being taken advantage of by someone who was supposed to babysit me, to perverted men in general, to an abusive husband, my granddad was always right there through it all to tell his hilarious perspective with intelligent humor that always made me realize I was not making good choices, or unfortunately someone else hadn't made good choices for me.

Challenges always show up. I can feel myself go to the path well traveled and start to let the devils' thoughts creep in. Using painful memories for me like I will lose my job and not be able to pay for this and lose it. Sometimes, bad things start to happen like my mood goes sour, and it causes distance in my marriage. Then thoughts creep in that he can't possibly love me like he claims to, and possibly could have already cheated, and I should watch myself. It's not until I sit back down with God that I'm reminded He will always provide, and this time, He gave me a faithful, wonderful man that loves Him just before me as he should. But his character is genuine like mine, and if I don't let crazy thoughts pop in my head, I can see that, and feel it. Over time because I have trusted and believed, those thoughts and feelings had reduced and almost went away, because I know what to do with them now. In replacement of them is a stronger and deeper love and relationship with God, and my husband.

My granddad didn't worry ever because he fully trusted God. And everyone that has this trust for their life and peaceful spirit does. How could you not want that? It's so hard, but you must start somewhere. I didn't have a clue. After reading one good book about the possibility of that freedom from a relationship with God, I had to keep reading and find it. I'm still learning every day and getting closer to that freedom each time. Challenges are still present, but I know how to handle them a little better every day.

CHAPTER 15

Are You Ready for Your Answers?

I've had three blood tests in a week to see if my baby is going to make it just to be told every time that I can just expect to have a miscarriage and go to the hospital if I start bleeding. Not a fun feeling of waiting for that, especially after celebrating your pregnancy and announcing it to family and our kids. At first my thoughts went to "it's over" to "God can do anything and can make it be just fine." So if He doesn't, there's a really good reason, like the next house is meant to be, but not this one. Or this job didn't need me, but the next one will, so I'll enjoy my free time until then with a boat.

If it doesn't turn out well, I'll cry, I'll be sad, but also I will be okay to wait for the right time. It won't be easy, but I'll ask Him for strength every day, and He will give it to me. Because no one is perfect, we all have bad thoughts, but I'll come back to Him, and He will show me the truth, again and again. People will think you've created this peace in your head because you've been through a lot, and you just want it so bad and possibly that you've lost your mind a little. I know because that's always what I thought of what seemed to be overly religious people at that time. Those people usually think there is no way peace like that can happen and no way you could talk to God. They probably also doubt He exists, whether slightly or strongly. And if you doubt at all you won't find it and you won't find

God and when or if you do, all those fears and doubts completely vanish from what you can hear and see and experience in your life.

November 15, 2020

He heard my cry for an answer. It's as if I had to write down that I would trust Him no matter what happened. After many weeks of being pregnant and not knowing if it was a normal pregnancy after my surgery, my HCG levels not rising enough and being told I would miscarry, after writing yesterday I took my youngest son to lunch as I usually do on Saturday, and that's where I started to receive the answer. I managed to wait for my husband to get off work, thankfully a little early, and we went to the hospital. The pain and bleeding kept getting worse, and they still couldn't tell where the baby was. Finally, it was confirmed about an inch in size, was approximately around a seven-week-old pregnancy lodged in my tube. What news to hear that our baby was there, but we would have to dissolve the pregnancy, or it would rupture my tube or even be fatal to me. I cried through both shots they gave me, feeling like I was aborting a life we were so joyous to have conceived. The scariest news was that if it happens again, they would have to surgically remove that tube, and that we may have to wait a while to try again. After trying to quickly recover from surgery to have this wonderful experience, for it to turn into a scary and uncertain situation, we left the hospital and didn't speak a word on the way home.

I have read much about demonic illnesses versus human illnesses, and it made me wonder. I read a story of a woman who was about to be admitted into a psychiatric ward because she would not consummate her marriage and began babbling as if she lost her mind at the mention of intercourse. It's one of Rebecca Brown's deliverance stories where she was able to find out the woman had several demons in her body controlling her, and the most powerful one had entered as her own father had sex with her when she was a child. Brown mentions several times that sexual abuse is one of the easiest ways for a demon to enter or to cause you harm from outside the body. Also those practicing witchcraft with a hatred for you can do the same.

At this very moment, all the horrible sexual abusive situations I've encountered flooded my mind, along with knowing certain people near my life, not in it but near it, that practice witchcraft. With all that I have learned, I now wonder, is this a case of human natural illness from my surgery? Do I need to pray for guidance and freedom of my past sexual abuse, or for the covering of my body for someone wishing to cause me harm? So I will seek answers this week while knowing I still have so much to be thankful for in my life.

True Faith Can't Be Faked or Forced

November 21, 2020

I watched a video of a woman passionately singing, then remembered another one of someone I know singing to God that I knew was a horrible person. Two totally different vibes. We can't deny it. Why try? The one who was horrible deep down inside still had a beautiful voice, just didn't roll so easy and draw you into what she's feeling with each word. The horrible one is more concerned with wanting you to think she's amazing. Maybe this is why really great artists are growing up often in broken homes that are troubled or have some kind of major setback. They hurt, and to feel it, they use this gift in a positive way to get through it. That positive dream sometimes turns into a burning desire that when anyone hears their sound, they feel that emotion. Wouldn't be unlikely they'd turn into a star with that kind of passion and sincerity. The horrible woman, not saying they can't make it to being a star, too, but you can still tell the difference. This one cares more about everyone telling her she's gorgeous and her voice is amazing and being directly in the center all the time. She usually bats her eyes when she talks to you and throws her hair around, trying to be cute while she's talking. It's obnoxious. But women like the one in the first video where her music is felt is gorgeous when she talks, and she's just enjoying life. Your opinions don't matter, and she doesn't waste her talent on caring. There is creativity in her. She enjoys experiencing God on her own when no one is watching. It's all about their relationship, not just looking like she's full of faith. The problem is once you learn that God only hears those who are sincere to Him because they love Him, not just looking like they do, always get noticed because that comes naturally. Just like I read only God's people can hear Him, this did make me nervous. I got even more nervous thinking that's how He can answer prayers. He only hears those that are connected over everyone else. Makes sense. Now I rack my brain with how can I be heard? But I then think of all the things I have overcome. To sit here with this beautiful view with this life after all those things, to be picked up from all that and beautifully placed on track, all while saying God is good through each time, but not even knowing Him, He does hear me. Better yet, He knew my heart, and still does.

Not because I've studied day after day to know Him because that's a fairly new thing for me I'm still working on, but because my intentions were always good. Doesn't mean I didn't do anything wrong, I did a lot of things wrong. But I felt bad if I did something and I hurt someone else. I take responsibility for what I did wrong. But the core inside respects what's right and what's wrong. Being a manager and having to be hard on people at times, say uncomfortable things, and even fire people, if your core is good, this can be hard. What's even harder is when they make you out to be the devil claiming all the things they did to get where they are were because of you. I was once called racist for firing someone of a different race than myself, which couldn't be further from the truth. Of course, it couldn't be related to poor performance. It had to just be hate. That hurt me bad. What if others believed it? The world will make you bitter if you let it. Don't.

Hurt is something I have always pushed down inside myself because I'm too strong for that. Yes, it's okay to be mentally strong. It's necessary to pull yourself back up. However, part of collecting all these negative toxic skeleton bones that eventually makes you a ticking time bomb is not dealing with the emotional aspect. It's okay to do that. I told myself all the time you got one day to feel bad, and then you need to suck it up so many times. Now I need to think so much through to clear it all out, it would take over a year or several. Emotions really do have to be worked through and felt to be yourself forever and not turn into a bitter soul that hates life. In a book that helped me mourn our recent loss, it took me to a place in the Bible that said predestined bodies in the womb basically meaning there's a reason that happened. It was predestined and a plan for a reason. Do you ever look back on your life's events and understand why something fell through? It wasn't meant to be, not for you, or not for something else. How much you trust and understand this clears your future for great things.

November 28, 2020

After many days trying to figure out what my lesson for this was I was finally told. Usually, I would say I'll ask God for the answer until I don't get my answer quick enough, then I'll convince myself to have faintly heard the answer I wanted to hear. But this was different. I felt it as if it was being told to me. It came out of nowhere when I stopped trying so hard to make my answer be what I wanted it to be. Because I realized you can't force faith or life. I soon began to learn that once I just listen because I genuinely want the answer to avoid hurt in the future, it comes to me suddenly. I just believe whatever I hear is the right answer even if it's not what I want because I realize my plan was already mapped. Often with these things sprinkled in that made me come back clinging to my faith. When I started really wanting this connection with God the most, and had control (somewhat) over my own life, I had the strongest urge to move to North Carolina out of nowhere. I used to say I was moving to South Carolina for the sun and sand nearby one day, but I never really believed I could! I knew if an opportunity presented itself, I would try. But I suddenly wanted a new life away from people that used, neglected, or physically hurt me. I wanted to be safe, free, and loved like never before. When my urge to leave got so strong, I felt a pull to South Carolina. When the opportunity for North Carolina dangled in front of me, I knew without any doubt God had thrown me my rope. It's amazing to think that leaving my entire family, hometown, friends, help of any kind with two young boys and an abusive husband didn't scare me, especially considering I was afraid of my own home with places to run to if I needed to. I asked myself several times if it was a good idea. My head said no, but my nerves were calm and excited, and my mind had already been made up. Now living this new life where I am free to be me and have fun and do whatever I want with someone who makes me feel safe 24-7, no questions asked. Loved like I'm precious, someone I genuinely have fun with and love to be with, I realized I was taught to have faith that God will place everything in line for you, but you have to take the steps He takes you to and to always respect them going forward.

In this pregnancy, I was counting ovulation days, praying for a boy, trying to predict what month to avoid certain horoscope signs that I didn't like, and planning around our trip in April. It all flooded my mind at the same time, and it was a strong message saying only He controls all of this, so stop trying. It became obvious to me that my lesson was to not even try to control my life. He can take that life; He can also make it so we couldn't have another child together at all. Makes things a little scarier than before. My immediate thoughts were what if I never get that experience? And just like leaping across the United States away from everything I knew and with someone I now know had let the enemy into my life. Because He said it was clear how I had to commit right now to accepting that possibility and committing to be okay with that if that's what God chooses, and that I will not waiver in my faith no matter what. That's hard. You think that's hard until you know that whatever is waiting on the other side you will love if you give Him the decision to make your reality.

December 3, 2020

Four days later and one tube shorter, if I ever felt challenged to stay faithful, it's right now. I wrote that no matter what happened, I knew my faith could not waiver no matter His choices, and I meant it. And I still feel it. But I still have the possibility to have a child.

What will I feel like if I lose the other tube? Can I stay steadily faithful and trust the plan? Somehow after everything I have learned and heard and been shown by the Spirit Himself, I think I can say yes. But it still hurts. Monday, I did my lab work. My hormone levels had dropped down by half. The doctor said that's great news, but I'm not yet out of the weeds. I felt good. He said next week it will flatline, and we can try again. Wednesday, however, normal day at first. Worked out at 5:00 a.m., made the bed, had coffee, got ready, went to work, and did great on a conference call I had been preparing for. Was proud of myself and feeling good. Suddenly all that changed in an instant, and I was doubled up in pain. Stuck in my office, sweating, could hardly breathe. Once I did get up going outside for fresh air, I sat down and couldn't get up again. People trying to talk to me, I didn't know what was going on. But I knew my right side hurt so bad, and that's where the baby had been. After calling the doctor and being told to come in right away, I asked someone to drive me there and was shocked when I couldn't even walk inside. She took me up to the ob-gyn where they took me in for a sonogram and found the now tissue in my tube had grown even bigger. Next thing I know, they are preparing me for emergency surgery to take the tube out. My heart sank as I thought about nothing but the fact that our chances of having a baby just got cut in half, followed by please let me get into surgery before my tube ruptures. Apparently, it had started to which explained the sudden agonizing pain. What do you want on the other side of this?

December 4, 2020

In the book *Held*, it speaks on how Jesus took human form to come to earth for approximately thirty-three years. He experienced hunger and thirst in the weaknesses of flesh and limitations. We as humans often don't want to accept those limitations and want to manipulate our reality or prayers to what we want. I really did this. I felt if I willed to become pregnant at the right moment and manipulated the situation, our baby could be the gender I wanted it to be, born in the month I wanted it to be. And in that, I believe God has shown me through this lesson my body has limitations that only He can control. When we found out it was ectopic, I prayed God would let it miraculously end up in the right place. After the first shot, they swore that would be it, and I wouldn't need a second one. After the second one, I knew we would get to try again in just a few weeks, and I would be fine. I tried again to be a bully in prayer to get what I wanted. When they said get ready for surgery, I still said I'll get pregnant on the other tube.

As I lay hurting a few nights after surgery, I became afraid. I felt pain all over my body, and my mind went crazy with bad thoughts about how it was an emergency surgery no one, including me, had time to prepare for. I hated that after midnight last night, the doctors and nurses stayed late because I kept the place open. What if they were already exhausted with all this kind of stuff from their long days? What if they botched me, and the pain is infection? The pain seemed to get worse, and all I could think of was prayer. I asked my husband to pray over me for the healing of all my organs and incisions. As he did, I felt healing and calmness and peace. I was able to relax the rest of the night. But I thought it could be even worse. I shouldn't be thinking about anything but being healthy. But I ran into the question, what do you want on the other side of this?

I was afraid to answer. Earlier, I would have said a little baby boy born in July or August or September with curly brown hair and green eyes, and my mind would have been flooded with memories I so badly wanted to have with my husband, with our kids, with our family, with our baby. But now I was afraid to answer. In going through the situation, rather than trying to skirt around it, you do learn to trust Him more and yourself less. He knows what you need or don't need, so how do I say what I wish to happen, but also give Him total control? Do I have to be weak and frail to be reminded I am not in control? How do I always remember that even when I feel strong and independent? In pain, instead of rushing through it, we must take the time to heal but also to feel, to feel the lesson, to feel the spirit with us, and to feel his presence through it. Suddenly then I knew the answer to what I wanted on the other side. It was just peace. Peace. To continue appreciating all the blessings God has given me so far. To be here to enjoy them and not to let anything disturb the peace I had been growing through my relationship with the Lord. To completely trust any and everything I need in my life will be provided at exactly the right time, that I needed to accept that I don't know what I need, but God does. To be patient and understand again whatever is on the other side I will love if I let Him take control because He knows me and my life more than I do. This reminded me of Matthew 14:22–36 where Jesus called Peter to walk on water with Him. When Peter got scared, he begin to sink, and Jesus said, "You of little faith." When we trust in Him, we can do great things, but when we stop believing, we sink. We can't live this life on our own. We must trust in Jesus, in the Lord, baptized by fire (*Prepare for War*, page 76).

January 17, 2021

I know firsthand how very difficult it can be to fully trust and understand. I feel as though I have been given yet another challenge from God to prove myself, and make the right decision for my life, and also to hear Him or not. This is one of my biggest challenges that again seems to come so naturally for my husband and bonus momma. Maybe it just takes practice.

Now in contemplating whether to stay in my current position at work that has many stressors or go back to a place that just a few years ago threw me out the door, but also gave me twelve great years before that where I fully enjoyed my job, by the way for much less money, on a thought or hope that my work-life balance will be much better.

When the offer came, I was so excited until she said the highest salary she could go. My mind immediately went to there's no way possible that I can do that. When that explanation was given to my husband, he said, "If you're going to make up your mind by yourself, you won't hear what God wants." Then when I tried to use my own knowledge again and showed him all the bills I currently paid, he said it didn't matter. If this is where you are supposed to go, God will make it work.

Have you ever turned something down because you didn't think it would work, but then afterward several other events happened that would have made it work? It was explained to me this is how faith is exercised and tested.

Even after much reading, the answer has not completely been made clear, Lord. I believe I heard You yesterday. Tell me this is what I prayed for. A better work-life balance also can't come with the same amount of money, I understand that. More than that, I'm scared they won't hold me in as high of regard as my current employers do. But could my miscarriage have happened to delay us for this change in our life for the possibility of what I prayed for? To have the ability to be a better wife and mother by way of more time and less stress.

When I thought the Lord was talking to me yesterday, I felt it in my heart, and then without anything in the forecast, it began to snow. It lasted only a few minutes. Is this a sign? I pray to you, Lord, for the peace of my decision to come to me very strongly and evidently to not be mistaken. You know more than I and can see our future. Please show me what Your will is so I can ensure it will be done. I must make a life-changing decision tomorrow.

CHAPTER 17

Who Could You Be If Encouraged?

January 23, 2021

My husband has reacted to situations in our life with a kind of faith I never knew. The more I heard his faith, the more I wanted it for myself as well. The more I read, the more I began to know that's entirely what faith is. God can make things happen that people who reason a lot or are only able to see what is have a very hard time understanding. I read about a lady today who called herself a puppeteer. She thought she was fully in control of her life. Every decision she had made on her career and husband so far had been great ones when it came to completing her own plans or her life. She was now pregnant and going to have a child until her plans were changed by miscarriage, and it was then that she realized she wasn't in control after all. That experience brought her to God, to have a relationship with the one that she now understands is in full control of her life. God uses these situations to get our attention to understand why it may not be a good thing in this moment of your life or not at all. Losing my job of twelve years suddenly when I felt the most valuable sent me to God for help and understanding. He, of course, caught me, and I never missed a beat. But a valuable lesson for many was learned in those moments to help me for the future.

Sarah conceived a baby at eighty-nine years old. She laughed when God told her she would. We often think there is no way a situation would work out but become impatient or think we need to take matters into our own hands and force things to happen, like puppeteers of our own lives.

Now more than ever, I am curious what God has in store for my/our life. I feel that the more I am able to understand that I don't know what's best for myself because I don't know what's in the future, nor do I know what amazing things God can do in my life that could be far better than I ever thought possible, the more I want to step back, relax, and let the master work. It's a peaceful thing to know all things will fall in place for the good. All you must do is trust your creator.

So today, I say God, let the decision be Yours of which job I take or stay with. Let my finances fall in line as You work on my situation either way. Let the miracle of extending our family be Your decision, in your time, because it will always be the right time and place. I trust You, Lord, because I know You will never let me down or leave me, and through everything, You will be with me providing lessons and blessings. I await my future with excitement.

I began reading because I was encouraged. I feel safe exploring and being myself because I am encouraged. I feel peaceful and not stressed because I am encouraged. Encouragement comes from true partnership, true love, true protection, knowing that whatever deci-sion I make with prayer that I have heard the correct one, that my husband will never tear me down during lessons, never blame me for troubles we encounter and always take them on as a team. I know I have a teammate who stands with me on earth through everything and a heavenly Father that stands with us guiding our way through encouragement and protection as well if we simply trust Him. I have also learned that when two genuinely good people find each other and declare to the Lord that they will do this life together with His guidance as a team no matter what comes their way, it's a magical thing with endless possibilities.

Have Your way with our life, Lord. I am so excited about what You can do.

In a book I was reading about when women pray, amazing things can happen when there seems to be no hope. And of those amazing things I read, I realized I already had experienced several on the list. Why couldn't it happen again and again? And the things I'm praying for today would be so much simpler than the things God turned around for me before I even knew how to pray for them, or better yet that I could. Coming out of so many horrible situations, having the confidence to leave my hometown and drive 450 miles and start over with no one but an abusive husband, two young boys, and a dog.

Being freed from abuse and all the blessings that came immediately after. Things being mysteriously sent to me at the right moment to help me on my way. A home selling days before foreclosure. These were all things that happened right on time because God had heard my cries when I didn't even know it or Him, really.

I can't imagine what could've happened if I had prayed for them also. Even if it would have just been the peace in my heart to know it would be okay and not have experienced the stress along the way I put myself through.

Let life be a journey and God be the guide.

January 31, 2021

This book started out as documenting my journey of learning faith and showing others as damaged and confused about faith as I was that it isn't crazy, that faith is real, and that a peace for you so amazing can be achieved if you run to God. Believe me, I work on this one every day of my life still. It is now turning into my real-life examples of how God is working in my life. After being told the job was mine, and even refinancing my house to accommodate the decrease of income, my husband and I prayed that if this move was not in God's plans that it be blocked somehow. To intervene if it wasn't in the path for the future God wanted for us. The very next week, I was called and told that training would be too difficult with COVID-19, and they had to take another candidate who had done the position before. That they really wanted my leadership experience, but this would be much easier since there was a travel ban. That wasn't a concern the previous week when she said, "I chose you after your first interview," went as far as to get a pay exception to go to the max for this position, and state that we would make a great team. So if God can answer in this manner to ensure we don't go down the wrong path or have any obstructions to the future He has in store for us, if we say, "I place this in Your hands and please let Your will be done," imagine what He can overcome to ensure you get that future. Again, I am even more excited. My life is wonderful as it is, don't get me wrong. I have the most loving, supporting, sweet husband, best friend, and partner in one, four beautiful children, a wonderful home that brings me so much joy, just enjoying the peace and comfort it provides our family, many family members and friends. We don't worry about our health, safety, or security. Definitely many things to be grateful for. But it took a very, very long journey to get here, and I aspire for much more. Of course, we want to extend our family and be blessed with another child that has our DNA mixed together, and I have always had dreams of a self-sufficient business that enhances my creativity and opens up my passion. I have many ideas of things I love to do, but what can we do that makes sustainable income that will take care of our family? This is now what I am praying to God for, as well as peace every single day.

Along the way being challenged to maintain that peace, yesterday, I encountered a situation that took me back to who I used to be. Hard-hearted, cut like a knife, hostile on the inside, don't get in my way. I couldn't believe how long I've worked on getting rid of this person, and one similar situation brought her back in a flash. The "I'm on my own," survival mode, "I don't care what I do to you to save myself." Here we are again.

All the years of someone in my face daily, disrespecting me, yelling in my face, threatening to hurt me. Hasn't happened since February 1, 2017, and now here it is, and my fist is suddenly clenched and so are my teeth, and I can envision myself taking a swing with this fist.

Being in an abusive situation daily, you learn ways to hold someone down or back. All care for what happens to them goes out the window, and you fight for your life. If a finger gets broken or a rib or anything else, you don't care at the moment because if you don't give it all your strength, it could be yours.

Ready to protect myself on command even through the night, just in case they wake up over top of you, grabbing your head to pound it into a wall or pulling you back and forth by the hair. I never slept all the way for years. Ready to react to save my already injured neck from years of abuse. I had tremors all through the night when I did sleep, and after being loved and safe for four years now, I thought she was gone for good. Here I am waking up in the middle of the night now several times and fantasizing about taking care of the one that threatened me, showing them they will never scare or touch me because I will always be ready. This, of course is scary. It dawns on me that the enemy is slipping back into my thoughts. I suddenly feel hard again. I suddenly do not feel loving at all. I suddenly feel skeptical of everyone and ready to strike at anyone who may threaten me at any given moment.

Lord, help me, I am so damaged!

I am brought to even this, God is using for my glory. Even a miscarriage, a lost job opportunity, and a spark of what I've worked to eliminate inside myself were done for a reason to use for His glory eventually.

I am also taken to Genesis 50:15–21 where Joseph told those who meant evil against him that he forgave them, and God turned it for good eventually.

Romans 8:28: "We know that all things work together for the good of them that love God, to them that are called according to his purpose even all of your situations."

February 6, 2021

The end of the story is planned. The end of the Bible was planned. The end of our stories are planned. There were women in the Bible who suffered with infertility that crushed them. They even conceived at odd times of their lives. Oddly enough so that their descendants would be on earth at the same time. Sarah gave birth to Isaac as an old woman, so he was on earth at the perfect time to marry Rebekah. Rebekah had fertility issues but eventually had twins, Jacob and Esau. Jacob married sisters who also had fertility issues but eventually gave birth to Judah whose tribe would eventually have Jesus, and the other gave birth to Joseph. All born exactly when they should have been.

Held by Abby Wedgewood: "God is not part of our story; we are part of his. He already knows everything about us. Even if we want something that is not in the plan, he may make it happen at the exact time that makes sense to his plan. Wait to see how your story ends… Faithfully trusting in Him!"

February 27, 2021

You get so caught up in life, don't you? I haven't written for a few weeks, and I was really craving to. All of a sudden when I was preparing to write today and trying so hard to relax and get in the right mindset to talk to God in a way that only He controls if He shows up fully or not. Sometimes He just watches, and you don't know if He's really there, but if you go deeper and deeper in your studies, sometimes He'll show up. I haven't written on pages, but for the last few times I did write, He didn't show up. Wars were in my head, but I put them there. After relaxing, I realized if my dedication and spirit are in it, God tells me every word. How did it stop or why?

In reflecting on myself, I realize every time I don't take the time to talk to God, I lose sight of where I'm going, where I should go, where I'm meant by God to go. Suddenly it came to my head a few days ago all the feelings I felt from the first few pages of this book. It was the first obvious time God showed up to me and to my life ever!

He was watching me for sure, and somehow, I knew He was there. I would be upset with myself that I had never heard from Him, and was starting to not believe those that said they did. Which side of that do you want to be on in life? Because the nonbeliever will never get to experience total peace like the ones they think are crazy! I admit sometimes I thought it. I would be juggling this crazy life, but still saying I believe in God and jealous of those who seem to just love life no matter what. To not be aggravated with others, but seemingly very happy. Nice no matter what. It was like someone was giving them all the answers in the life test. The bad things still happened in their lives, but it was always saved by something else later, and they didn't worry in the meantime.

So I haven't made time to talk to God really in about a month, and in that small time, I forgot what life was about. Or life consumed me. So much so that I forgot to be present in life. I had the job scare that I thought I might be going somewhere else for a better work-life balance that mysteriously changed at the last moment. I was upset and relieved, all at the same time. Upset because in my head, it would be easier and make my life better. I was uneasy because it meant going back to a company that tossed me in the trash and leaving the one that picked me up and treated me so good right after, even if it was a stressful mess by nature.

After losing a baby, and before the better distractions such as visiting loved ones and going on a mini vacation with my soulmate directly after losing power for an entire weekend, it dawned on me this is just life, a few great weeks, a few really frustrating weeks, a few busy weeks, but it's all distractions! Once I got distracted, I looked back and realized I was worried, anxious, and nervous. I started worrying I will never fix this broken building I'm in. I may never have a baby with my soulmate. I am angry because of X, Y, Z. But when I started craving this moment and reflected and realized this was all from the enemy because I was distracted, this happens all the time. What changes? I was starting to make early appointments on Saturdays which I wouldn't before so that I didn't limit my time with God or make it feel rushed. So I wouldn't have to force relaxation, but rather enjoy it. I'd make grooming appointments or facials for me to relax, but I'd speed up my time with God sometimes to just an hour. So I was distracted. When I look back at those weeks, I was not a great wife, mother, or even employee. People talk to me, but my heart wasn't truly in it. I was distracted with all my worries and concerns. I was singing songs about how God takes care of everything for you on the way to work and at church, but I was worrying about everything in my life again. Do I want to get so distracted, I don't feel joy and peace? I don't really listen to engage with others, especially those I love so much. I began to worry again that I will never have a career that is mine alone. Writing, flipping houses, somehow becoming an artist because I want to have the time to do those creative things I love so much. I was craving to come back to peace and let God tell me what to do. How could I feel anything at all about not getting a job when I prayed to God to block the opportunity if it wasn't meant for our family?

How could I worry about not possibly getting to experience having a baby with my husband when I'm praying God to put the proper pieces of my life together only if it is in His will? How contradictory is that? It's so hard to fully trust though, but it's what faith is. You have to know and trust and believe and thank Him without yet seeing anything. I went on a weekend trip with my husband to slow down and remembered what life is actually about. I began to have more peace, and I prayed for God to just get me back on the right track and talk to me. I came home from my trip to a birthday present from my sister with a note that says, "Hopefully this will help with writing your book." The box had a diffuser with oil and a book on assisting with writing and a journal that said, "Follow your dreams." I'd forgotten so many things. I forgot I wanted to write a book. I totally forgot about the first few pages where God Himself showed up to the meeting and wrote on my page that if I spent time with Him, He shows up to speak. I write it down, and it becomes a book. Not just for me but for others to learn. I didn't know if I remembered all that, but when I wanted to go look it up on my first journal, my pen pushed so hard, the words just came to my head. I remember the first time that happened and remembered it was so obvious to me it was the Holy Spirit. I hadn't had an encounter like that in a while, but I begged God to show up this morning, and He did. I haven't read one of my books yet this morning, and my head is full of so much, I can't write it down fast enough. And I know some of it wouldn't even make it to this chapter because I will have forgotten it before my hand wears out.

That first time God showed up, I honestly forgot I had ever wanted to be a writer. It's like God opened a wall of my authentic self that He created to show me who I was meant to be, and it was me at seven years old. I just remember feeling at seven years old, I could do so many things when I grew up. I wanted to write a book so bad. After hearing certain books and reading my first interesting book of Shiloh the dog, I wrote a book about a dog. Not super creative, but it was the beginning of the journey. I also remember thinking I could build myself cool things like a playhouse if I could gather the right materials, but was obviously never able to. When I started working with my granddad in the woodshop, I wanted more and more of that. I would go to their house and run straight out to the shop if that's where he was. I loved to learn those things, but also to watch my granddad's brain. It was that of a creator also, and definitely an artist. He drew on every restaurant placemat he went to and then gave the intricate picture to the waitress. My mamaw and I were always impressed with it every single time. His brain fascinated me and reminded me of an even more excelled version of my own brain. Life always wins over just letting you freely do what you love. But how distracted do you get and how long do you let the enemy talk to you is the question. Because he will take the first opportunity you provide. You stray and don't want to take any risks because of worrying. As I relaxed that first morning, God showed me who I could be and reminded me of what he had given me a passion for from a young age. Instead of hearing it could never happen, I saw pictures of what else could happen if I believed in what he told me in the beginning of my journey. He also showed me what could build upon my dreams, even after just writing. The lifestyle that surrounds writing and how it was so fitting for me and a lifestyle I would truly enjoy. Getting in time with myself and creating a space where creativity can grow. That's so up my alley. Building my relationship with God and possibly even being able to help others build their relationship with God so He can truly show them what their life is meant to be. Where do people go that get distracted or are taught to stay distracted? They believe all the worries they hear because the enemy keeps them there. They believe this is all there is to life and remain frustrated all their life that they may make bad choices and even turn to serious drugs or lack of self-care and even sometimes die young but always miserable or disturbed at least. Because there is only one way to happiness. I have seen it several times! It used to be all around me. I hated it, but some of it caught on. I still had my optimism, but I had to defend it hard when it was always shot down! Now I share my space and time with those that know the peace secret also and were not trying to screw it up for each other. The uneasy ones make it challenging for us, especially those with a history of having to be tough. Comes back quick, and you'll feel bad about it later, so that's why it's so important to refill yourself as often as possible with peace that only God can offer. I can't even begin to think of what the world would be like if everyone found the peace secret. Anxiety would be low, and we would all be living lives we authentically love.

One of the most amazing things about my first encounter with God is that sometimes it would take forever to talk to God before I received an answer. I had to get up early to have enough time, but eventually I couldn't wait to, and I am a horrible morning person. And then I would start reading something for inspiration, which eventually you just can't get enough of also and you don't want to stop. You don't want to stop because you learn so much, you start feeling it more and more, and you like it. You start to feel those pieces of peace everyone has been talking about, and they look so relaxed, not a care in the world. These are the people I once thought were weak. They were so peaceful, it was annoying. It had to be an act. No one is that peaceful. They're just pretending. But when His word starts touching you to be peaceful, it doesn't seem so stupid anymore, and a group you once would never be close with are suddenly the only people you want to be around. "But you can't" is what God told me. Because those that have not yet discovered His peace are the ones who need help. The ones you used to be so very close to that suddenly don't want to be around them again because you're finding God. So when you have the meetings with God and He talks quickly, like today, I know I'm on the right path. I know if I get busy, I won't hear Him as easily or as often. In last Wednesday night's service, the speaker said finding God is like you start dating Him, and you can't wait for your weekly date. You even look forward to it, and that's the case for me. He said your feelings change, and suddenly you never want Him to leave. I'm thinking the only way I could ever under-stand this is because of exactly how I found love with my husband. I had such a hard heart from everything I had been through. I had moved over four hundred miles away from everything and everyone I knew because I wanted to raise my kids differently. I didn't want them in a drug-infested town where everyone knew each other, and someone dragged everyone into the crowd. I did this with a man that scared me every day. A man I didn't know if he might kill me one day. On purpose, but more than likely accidentally. And it was only one year into it that was the case. I blacked out three times in two weeks from abuse, but when I came out of my last episode I said this is not what I moved here for. I really wanted to enjoy life more than ever. I did, with the help of so many angels that were put in the right place at exactly the right times. Thank you to my close friend that showed me a way out of that life. You know who you are, and yes, you were one of those strange people I couldn't understand. She cared enough for other people that she took interest in my life when she didn't know me that well. But that interest got enough visibility that she was able to see I needed a push, and I needed help now. It is only because she noticed, helped, and pushed me that we got out safely. She took me to all the right places and asked the right questions to keep me from spinning, afraid to get the result I wanted because what if it turned out bad for me. If I had him arrested and he gets out of jail tomorrow, I don't want to know what will happen to me.

But she kept me brave, picked up my kids, did nothing but talk positive and tell me I will be fine and God's got it. She could have been upset and said, "I don't have time to deal with her problems. I've got five kids [and she did] and homeschooled them all." Why would she be interested in helping me? But she loves people because she loves God. There were so many other people that got me through this rough, scary, but exciting time. Exciting because I got to learn what it is like to be free, to be me again. I would think of things I was not allowed to do or buy before, and then say why not? Oh, right, that's not a rule anymore. In this new group of friends I had, it was easy to see who really cared. But there was one that truly cared the most. Even when I was saying, "You're a man, and you're not going to make me fall for that trick again. You can be real sweet and learn me, and eventually start setting rules and controlling me again. I don't think so."

He didn't care about that. He just cared about me. If I needed a ride to rent a car or go search for a new one in another state, he would offer to watch my kids while I was there, and most importantly, I felt comfortable letting him too. He amazed me with how he would respond to me and my crazy reactions. I wouldn't even let him pay for anything, even lunch at work because I am an independent woman that will give you no reason to owe you anything. Our story should be a book by itself. It was so amazing. His book on it would be a lot more entertaining. He once told me after we started dating when I was having an "I don't need anyone" episode, "I'm going to let you get yourself together tonight, and I'll see you tomorrow." This was after I had yet another meltdown after weeks of having fun together and I suddenly said, "I can't do this again, and I don't want another relationship."

This, of course, wasn't the first one, so he was so used to this by now. After a while, he just said, "Forget it. You know this relationship is worth it, and so do I. Now get yourself together." But every time that happened, he would say something to the tune of "I understand why you would feel this way, but I care so much about you. I just want to be in your life in some way, even as a friend, so don't shut me out." He could have said, and this is what I was expecting, "Okay, bitch, thanks for wasting my time and not even giving me anything." But he was still caring and loving and didn't even care about selfish needs at all. I will write that book one day, too, because it's beautiful, the way we found love in each other. But the point is that I really looked forward to being around him to the point I wanted him with me day and night and felt alone without him. Even if I got scared and lashed out to see how he'd react, expecting him to show me the signs of why I wouldn't want him, he never did. In fact, I felt more safe because he'd hold me through anything, even when I didn't deserve it. The night I knew I was all in and loved him was when I was being independent, putting together a firepit, and could hear him making me laugh in the background, but he wasn't there. I was laughing, and

I thought, *How in the hell did this happen, girl? We were solid. No way in hell any man's getting us again.* But somehow, I felt peaceful about it, and terror came to me when I thought about life without him. I knew I was on the right path when the speaker said it, and I thought in my head, *Yes, I don't want to be without God. How do I do more than date him?* When he compared this to dating his wife and wanting to marry her, then comparing that to my own experience with falling in love, I got it. I knew when he said it also, that's right where I am with God. I've heard him and now know it's the way. How do I get there?

I couldn't wait to ask that this morning, and right away, He spoke before I could crack a book. I was writing, and the pen hasn't stopped. The first thing I heard when I thought how do I get time to do this all the time, what is in my way of total peace, I thought my job, and I immediately heard "What are you going to do about it?" Then I took the crazy dogs in the yard and thought, *This is what I love to do every day, God, have always wanted to do and loved, but it's not possible alone. I can't make any money at this.* Then I suddenly realized just then I let the enemy in my thoughts, but I noticed so quickly. Because of that, I was able to control my mind and let God's word take over again and laughed at the enemy for trying. God says I can, and this is who I am meant to be, so I can! My conversation then continued. So what's the plan, God? How can You help me control my mind all the time and just talk to You directly, and how can I be this person doing what I love and still paying my bills, Lord? I'm so excited to see what You can do. Please don't let me get lost. That dream is so much better. I know You let me see it and feel it for a reason. How do I follow? Will you wear a yellow shirt or something and use a microphone or megaphone, please? I'm hardheaded! You know this! And I'm tired of learning the hard way, Lord. Open my ears and my eyes. Put it right in front of me to keep going. And I heard, "I've got ya!"

God will place those people in your life to provide encouragement from Him, and sometimes if you listen, He can encourage you, directly speaking into the spirit He has placed within us. Who is He telling you to encourage? It may be what they need at exactly the right moment and the way He chooses to use you to fulfill your purpose. If you let Him.

What Will He Tell You if You listen? I Am a Writer

March 20, 2021

I asked the Lord this morning why can't I be peaceful. When I tried to truly relax, things are still sent to my head that are not peaceful! I will admit that as I study, those thoughts are easier to turn off, but how do I just not have them? They could be in the form of having anxiety that something could happen to someone you love, or that earwax is a bug. We talk ourselves into some crazy things, don't we? The enemy can put a thought in your head that makes you believe your spouse is cheating on you and give you signs that aren't even accurate. How many times have you yourself been accused and their facts are all off-the-wall, yet seem that they could have somehow made sense? Sometimes a narcissistic person can make you believe you did something you didn't even do yourself. The people that let those thoughts continue to linger go further and further convinced. Sometimes when someone is already convinced, that's probably when a paranoid feeling from the enemy takes over, and he wins. Sometimes that voice wins so much so that we talk it into existence. Have you ever been accused of something so much, you think, "I might as well do it, because they are convinced I am already"? But what if instead you have no fear and say, "I know who this is, and you have no reign here. I know you're a fraud, and my God has me covered, but also know that you are. I know this now after all that has fallen into place for me. For me to be who I am and know how to combat that, but I have also been able to see and witness those that really have no fear no matter what comes their way because their faith is that strong. It doesn't happen overnight, but I have seen the change and progression in myself along this journey.

My job is very stressful, and things that need to have attention can follow you even on a Saturday, and it often does. As I'm enjoying the fire in the living room and reading and writing, enjoying my Saturday morning, it happens again. My thoughts usually go to *It's my weekend, and I can't even get a break or relax or get away from the problems I worked through all week long already.*

Sometimes I had even thought of ignoring it. However, as my faith grows, I understand that even this is a blessing. To have people count on you so much and need your patience and guidance is a gift God has blessed me with. It is easy to take for granted at times, especially when it makes pouring into yourself a challenge. But now I understand if I think things through and do the right things in planning and communication, it will all work out for the better. But I must believe that thought. There's no faking it. Mindset is extremely important as well. We must consider who is on the other side and what they are depending on us for. So instead of ripping things apart, we must depend on each other as a team. And just like that, an example is given to me right in my face as I'm writing this with a lesson for my new leaders.

Leadership was just discussed in church. The position I'm in currently requires a lot of leadership, somedays more than I feel I have to give. Leadership really is something you must develop. So is faith. His answer to my question was just like your life. Do not be afraid if you know that I've got you. But that's what I'm asking about, Lord. How do I never have those bad or challenging thoughts even if I shut them down fast? I don't want them at all. This is really where I am on my journey. I've never been here before. Every day must be peaceful was what I received. You must take it one day at a time and live in the moment. If you want everything to fall in place for your life to fulfill yourself, be where you are, learn, and grow others where you are, and you'll get to where you want to be. You can see all over your life where you're not living in the moment, especially at work, when you want to relax but can't with kids or responsibilities. It's so easy to slip back in the day to day. Go through motions and not fully care or just want to survive or get through the day. But what would happen if we fully lived, even in all of those difficult scenarios? We so often skip over the little things that have big results. Listen closely, fix the small things before they turn into big ones. They may be aggravating to deal with, but if you do, they will be solved quicker than not dealing with them in the moment or worse, not at all. This goes for everything in your life, but if you keep God in the loop of your life and how it's going and where it's not, He will show you exactly how to get to that perfect peace. This was my lesson today on that question.

April 2, 2021

I am a writer. I got my coffee this morning, and right away, I heard, "I am a writer. Say it yourself." I instantly repeated in disbelief. Then my mind quieted down, and all these thoughts came to it. Heat pack on my neck again to relax, up at 6:00 a.m. because I'm excited for my Saturday dates with God. An experience where I feel my spirit communicating to God quicker and quicker and more distinct each time. In the beginning and my whole life before that, I said I have no gifts. God does not talk to me. These people are making it up! And now I believe had I known I needed to study Him for those experiences, I would have started so much earlier. Now I know when things start to go wrong and I begin to get stressed or mad, they'll go right again when I listen to how to handle life and everything to say and do, then everything falls into place. I consider myself a smart woman. By no means was it easy only having eight years of school out of twelve. I tell people this now, and they don't believe me. I lost big years, middle school, the basis for high school, and junior and senior year. Go to high school without middle school, then bam, you're a freshman that really doesn't know anything. Trying to fit in on top of it all, so I studied everything. If someone said a word I didn't know or understand, I came home and looked it up. I still do this, but it gets on a higher level every time. Then when you're comfortable and excited for junior year after the hard work is done to catch up, it's over. So then work and studying everything and everyone again.

So yes, I consider myself a smart woman well-earned. I quickly see that these examples are similar to faith. We don't know all God's ways and love for us, or that these experiences can happen in order to really guide you to the life you want. It's actually so easy. He tells you what you maybe forgot inside if you listen. I am a writer.

The first time He told me that was amazing. It's the beginning of the book, and I've mentioned that experience before, but I had forgot. When I heard this, and it was inevitable God was talking to me, I was so amazed. All these thoughts came back about when I was little learning to write and I've always said as I was growing up I'd write what I thought would be a book about the crazy events of my life one day. There's still time, and I am planning on it. It will be a wild one. But now that I'm here, I realized God had not led me long enough to where my writing would show the result. But still working on it, right before your eyes. I believe I'm writing this for a reason, but I constantly ask myself, where do I stop, Lord? Sometimes I get so excited to type it up but keep being told to write.

At the church where I go, the speaker that night said, "Just wait." He said God is telling me to wait and show and tell someone how to wait. The pastor said I don't need to wait for me. God is telling me to wait for those that need to hear it. I had so many emotions on those words because of things I wanted so badly to come into fruition. It's amazing how and when God will speak to you if you listen. Maybe it's not in your own head but in someone else's words. My dream when He said it was my husband by my side at church holding me, two kids on each side of us and a beautiful baby we were all kissing on, praising God together in the middle. To be able to be peaceful and relaxed, be who I am meant to be waking up at 6:00 a.m. to write about the Lord and free to write His words, be a wife and a mother, still financially assist my family to maintain a comfortable life, and walk every day of my life with the Lord guiding me to get there.

This is crazy to me because all my life, I didn't know what to pray or how, but anytime I saw 11:11 on the clock, I prayed for the same thing. Just this: I wish for a happy, healthy life, and God's guidance to get there. Guess what, I saw 11:11 all the time. It almost seemed on purpose. This was the one thing God did and put in my head to get me through the bad times. I had no idea who He really was, or that He even existed at all, yet felt compelled to ask Him for this every time I saw 11:11.

I want to end this when and how God tells me. Seems he's telling me I'm a writer, and when I show the world the blessings He has for me, you will be able to line the dates of my pages with events in my life. My scars will be researchable such as a tubal reversal, a removal, and things that were going on at work. Eventually I will also be able to record my husband and our family that's now extended, praising together, and the record of the birth of our child. But, God, how will they know when I wrote the pages for sure and didn't make them up? He said, "Then we're finished until the next one, right?" Wow, God, that's pretty brave. I put this out to the world before we know if my blessings will come true, and He said, "Do you trust Me? Maybe blessings will come quicker than you think, so get it out there. Keep writing about what's happening, and by the time editors are done with this, You have number two ready."

I'm a writer.

Lead On

April 3, 2021

I was led on a journey by my phone, literally wandering around for about thirty minutes looking for my phone. The whole time, God's talking to me in my head, and honestly, I thought I was going crazy, flooded with thoughts that flowed so fast, I couldn't keep up. At one point, I even said, "Okay, God, hang on. I'm kinda looking for my phone because You told me to watch a video this morning. Can You help?"

He was leading me all over the place to look for my phone, and while I got frantic, He was saying, "People won't believe you. They may even talk badly about you, say you're crazy, bring up bad things you've said or done, and things you didn't even do. But you must move forward. Ask difficult questions because you are receiving them." I was getting kind of scared, and then He said, "Your phone is under your bed pillow. Can I not help you get through it?" And that's where it was. This is not somewhere I usually forget my phone. Okay, I understand. Lead on!

April 24, 2021

Peace means that you can recall or be recalled to a person that hurt you, maybe that always hurt you not just sometimes, and know there's a story of hurt associated with that memory, but you don't even care to let it into your brain anymore. There was a time when this person or moment was mentioned that what they said to you, what they did to you, and how it made you feel instantly reappeared, including the feelings that came along with it. Maybe you suddenly felt hatred or frustration for that person that took away your peace. A parent, spouse, friend, coworker. For me, every time my ex-husband was mentioned, I saw a demon-like face that would hold me down, grit his teeth at me with glaring eyes that really scared me. When I started having a quest for my relationship with God, when he was mentioned, it took much longer for me to recall any situation, and it was much fuzzier of a memory. He was mentioned to me by my husband recently, and I didn't even care to drum up discussion about the experience. I could hardly think of what that demon-like face looked like that I feared so much. I have plenty of those memories, but God showed me why I needed all of it. Had I never had those memories, I'd never realize the beauty of peace. Never crave peace so much like someone who lived off four hours of sleep at night, was always broke, plenty of beer and cigarettes in the house, and scared for the inevitable fight that will come out by the end of the night no matter what I said. The nights you can go to sleep peacefully is an anomaly, and it scares you even more for the next morning.

We all have a story like that somewhere, and some people are so unfortunate to have a story like that with just about everyone they know. Unfortunately, I was on that path. But what happens when you live with the very person that can give you peace instead? I truly didn't know that was an option! That's what I thought before. But now I know it's true, so I laugh instead of crying or getting angry. Peace comes from knowing your husband will love you like God does. That on your worst days together you feel bad for each other before you even want to say something you think might hurt them. Or if you do, it wasn't intentional, and you're truly sorry for it. Keion Henderson once spoke about mind control and acting like Jesus. He gave a verse where Jesus once said, "Mimic me." He spoke about how your mind can talk you into anything, making up stories that hurt your future if you believe them and let them take over. But I know how your mind can talk to you from things that have happened from the past. Things you don't even have to experience again, shouldn't that give you peace? What if every time you were told you're beautiful, you remember words you used to hear, like "You have a messed-up face." But when one and even worse both people in a relationship grow up thinking this is love and it's acceptable from what they saw, it becomes normal. When the peace and love of God is not in both sides of a marriage, the opportunity for evil to divide and grow is easily present. I'm just like you, and so many others. Or I was. If someone would've told me here's the guide to peace, I would have taken it any day, but they didn't. Why? Because they don't know, or if you do encounter those that do know, they can just seem annoying when you don't understand. But they are still caring toward you no matter what because they are peaceful, and they really and truly want you to be. God's people want everyone to find what they have found in Him. Because we know God is truly love, and He wants you to mimic Him. He knows you feel some type of way inside about those people that hurt you, but he says your mind is too valuable to start that fire with bad memories because when your mind is on fire, you can't hear me. The desire to be mad or frustrated or carry hate diminishes once you feel the love of God, and it becomes more difficult to care about all those unnecessary feelings that only harm you.

May 30, 2021

It's been about a month since I last wrote. But in studying the guidance of God and following His guidance as it comes to me, He has given me yet another task, or what I believe to be my next blessing to fulfill my desires in life. If you are wondering about the many ways in which God can speak to you, the guidance can come in many forms or sources if you are open to believing and listening. I've mentioned many times the stress of my current job and company just as is the nature of the industry itself. Many times, I have applied for other positions in frustration and at the very beginning of the year was even offered a position back with a company I knew very well. I prayed over and over that God would tell me this was the right direction. Should I go back to the company that once kicked me to the curb after years of faithful service, hard work, and dedication for a large pay cut, or stay where I am, where I'm very stressed, not much free time, but making great money, feeling very valued, and working very hard to improve the building, and maybe closer than I think in actually achieving that? I put it in God's hands, and after talking to my bonus mom, the question came up. What I would do if I didn't take it? I said out loud to God if this isn't the right opportunity and You intend for me to stay, I will, pay off all my debt this year early, and look for a way to open my own business, work for myself, or find something I can do that allows me to transition out respectfully, and gives me the time to write full-time. Eventually, take care of my family and home much better, including the child the Lord will eventually give my husband and me. After being told I had the position, I heard nothing for a week. Upon calling and questioning, I was told I was the best candidate, and my leadership experience is what they wanted, but they couldn't offer to me because of COVID-19 and travel restrictions for training. Odd since the week before I was told it was mine. I was positive the Lord blocked it and said, "You need to go the other route." The route to complete fulfillment. Okay, Lord. What is that? After I paid off all my credit cards and debt, a few months later, I was reading one morning when a Post-it note fell out of my book that said "Keion Henderson."

I pulled him up and randomly picked a sermon that ended up being about fulfillment, taking risks when others won't, believing in yourself, and trusting in God's plans for you no matter how big they seem. An ad kept blaring through about taking the leap of entrepreneurship with genuine people giving success stories! I signed up.

After the free class, I was given the urge to sign up for a three-day workshop. At the three-day workshop was the opportunity to continue investing in the education to basically be a franchise using their successful systems as your own, and once again, I was urged to take an expensive leap of faith. After bringing my husband in the loop, he had no doubts as well. So I found myself engaged in many hours of online training and focused to make this work and go somewhere, neglecting my writing. You gave me timelines? And I kept seeing the freedom to be a full-time author after establishing a business, exiting the workforce gracefully, preparing someone to take over what I worked very hard to put together, and eventually creating financial stability and freedom for our family, while also doing amazing things in the community like using our business to find ways to house the homeless as my husband and I have always talked about doing. Am I on the right track, God?

I know You use persistence to show me the way. Please show me this week all I need to see to know I'm following Your plans for me, and confirm my thoughts that I believe I'm hearing from You.

June 13, 2021

Over the past two weeks, my coaches have relentlessly called and pushed me forward. We set up and established our business name officially, and I have over the past few weeks asked myself the same questions. Is this what I'm supposed to be doing, God? Every time I spend money on something for the business and I get uneasy, it is followed by a peace that says, "Isn't this what you asked for?" Of much that is given, much is required. I'm also reminded of the day I wrote His words, "Do you trust Me?" Once I am peaceful about my next step, persistence quickly follows. The question of why are you doing this entered my mind before the peace comes. Is it for the right reasons, and it is. When I was younger, so many of the things I did and kept myself crazy busy for was for people to think and see how good of a person I was. I believed I had to do elaborate things for others to be viewed as a great person. I even believed I needed to do elaborate things for my children for them and everyone else to believe I was a great mother. At that time, I had not yet heard the word of God speaking to me as I do now, but I can imagine if I did, He would have asked me the same questions. Why are you doing this? What is your intention? Unfortunately, those I did things for did not react the way I wanted them to. They may have praised me for how wonderful everything was, but they abused my kindness to get things they wanted and took advantage of my hospitality and efforts. My intentions were in the right place, but my direction was not from God. When you do for others, it does not need to be publicly. In fact, the Bible tells us about how God rewards those who give in private. My heart was pure and good, but I didn't have to try so hard and needed to spend much of those efforts talking to God and learning the scriptures and His word instead of making myself crazy. This is truly the way He speaks and guides us, and that's why it is so important to know His word. His guidance often comes from scripture, and if the guidance you hear is contradictory to His word, you are not hearing guidance from the Lord at all. The guidance I continued to hear and see in this moment in my life continues to focus on "Do not worry, I am here. Stay focused on me to follow and reach your blessings. This is what you asked for. Follow me. God provides."

June 19, 2021

I asked God this morning, "Are these my thoughts or yours, God?" He said, "Our thoughts because we are one. I am in your soul, and our spirits are one." I asked many questions this morning as I felt so stressed and tense.

How will I ever get this building at work stable with people quitting and staffing issues every day with COVID-19, and at the same time start up this business I've invested so much in, and what if it fails? I NEED time to myself I'm just not even getting. I need time with just my husband, time with just my kids, time together as a family. I need time with you God also, time that I want more of every single day. How can I get more time, Lord, please? I really want to know how to get to the end by getting through all of this.

The first thought that came to me was baptism. The Lord has been telling me to be water baptized since last year this time, maybe even earlier. But with coronavirus, I was unable to have it done. It seems the church might be doing baptisms again in August. I really want to do it. Actually, I know I have to do it because I have been told repeatedly. The key is persistence and resistance. The Lord took me to Keion yet again. I felt like the sermon I was taken to was for me. It was called he's a promise keeper.

This is how the Spirit talks to us.

CHAPTER 20

His Timing Is Everything

July 24, 2021

Again, it has been about a month since I've last wrote, and I feel so lost. Not sure exactly even where to start. My stress levels trying to start a new business on top of a very stressful job, balancing my family, financials after just cleaning up debt, only to put myself back in it, for financial freedom seems to not be making sense, repeatedly not conceiving, and more than anything, no space, time, and a cluttered mind.

I do the right things. Should I have pushed more on my writing versus the business? Should I have found a less stressful job when I paid down all my debt instead? Everything was saying to me to start this business to create the freedom and stability we have been looking for. Now I'm begging the Lord to help me figure out how the heck to get there. Time doesn't seem to be on my side.

Without storms, you take things for granted. You've been through more than this. God doesn't waste pain on people He doesn't want to promote. The devil stops progress with negative thoughts. This is what I heard, along with again this is a blessing. The ability to even have the faith, courage, strength, and financial ability to attempt other options is a blessing in itself.

July 31, 2021

All my answers came much later. All your life, things were easy to go the wrong way and keep doing the wrong things. It's not until you put your mind in the right places that it got so challenging. Why is that?

Because the enemy didn't need to challenge you, you were going the right way according to him. Your own life was doing his dirty work. There was no need for intervention.

This was my very first thought today. Once again, I was reminded in several ways that when I tried to take control, the enemy began to speak and say, "I don't have time to connect with God." As always, that's when everything falls apart again. This week at church, I was reminded that my head and my heart have to match, and my head and my mouth have to match. I can't just take the wheel and say, "This is going to happen come hell or high water if I think about it hard enough." I have to believe it and know it to be true, or God reminds me I'm not focusing on Him and His guidance again.

This is the most difficult thing for me for sure! Right next to patience, ask anyone that truly knows me. Usually because I have so many things to do, mainly because I have always had so many dreams and aspirations. I've always thought there was something special inside me, something I wanted to give to the world, but couldn't figure out what it was.

I truly believed I could do so many things, and when I tried, I did them well. One of my only fears in life was what if there's not enough time for me to try all the things I want to try, experience all the places I want to, or I don't get to make a difference somehow? Time. Time has always been my enemy.

Ecclesiastes 3:1: "There is a time for everything, and a season for every activity under the heavens."

So now with trying so hard to get the things God has told me He has in store for me, how on earth could I wait? Glimpses of a possible future that's better than I could ever have planned, and I'm so excited, but when it doesn't happen or it feels like it's getting too difficult or I can't do it, I question. But I always get brought back to

God. I remember how it got so hectic last time. I prioritized Him on a number bigger than one. Now the times I am reminded on what happens when I stray get closer and closer in between the times I forget, which keeps my faith getting stronger all the time. I don't have as much work to do to get back on track, and I get a little further each time. When I start to lose sight of God again, my head clutters, and I can't relax.

I'm reminded of God's time and how I have seen it work in so many wonderful and large ways. For my husband and I both to decide to exit toxic marriages at the very same time and move from opposite ends of the eastern side of the country, both apply for the same job to get us there, be the exact two people they choose to fill only those two available positions, to get along so well during such a large process of starting a building and making it so easy to do together, to fall madly in love with each other, have two boys and two girls stairstepped, both oldest's names start with a D, both youngest's with a K. People have told us we had to have planned our kids perfectly, and it makes me laugh. Then suddenly I'm displaced at work and considering taking a job within the company in Florida just to keep my job.

Once again, the enemy stepped into the story. Time is a thief, but it's beautiful to watch everything grow. One of my employees texted me that this morning. Odd? No, I'm back to following the Lord's guidance. That's when you get exactly what you need when you need it, and don't worry. You don't have to find it. It will be waiting for you. I have always prided myself on being someone who can always makes things happen. I start to get frustrated when I can't with the things I now want, things I've been told I would get, so why am I forcing it? Timing! God's timing is right on time. So while it's getting frustrating, I'm getting distracted and pulling away.

The rest of that story is even all God at the right moment again, and I didn't even know it. So this horrible thing happens. I have exited a toxic marriage, found the man I was supposed to be with, and now we may get separated! We might have to wait on one of us to be able to transfer again maybe a year later? Travel back and forth? No. Okay, then the alternative is to lose my place of employment for the last twelve years and a career I worked so hard to build up and love so much. All for a man I've known for two years. I've been fooled before, many, many times. When it all got to be too much, I went to lunch with my husband's aunt who is a blessing to the world, and as I mentioned previously, she brought me a book, *The Power of a Praying Woman*. I left lunch that day and went and bought a Bible off the words she spoke to me, that God will step in and take care of the problem if I ask Him to. If I let Him.

My exact thoughts were it seems to be making all of them so peaceful anyway. I'll give it a try. And I read them both together. I was always so refreshed afterward, and I began to believe He would take care of it all. What I have not yet mentioned is I was immediately given an opportunity to stay with the company I knew so well, to stay in my comfort zone. I got the call for the interview in Florida from a GM who remembered I had worked with his wife in Ohio when they were there many years ago.

The fact I had so many connections like that alone within the company made me scared for how I responded to him. After his sentence was over telling me he knew I was displaced and on a tight timeline, with only a few weeks left to secure a job before losing my career, and that he'd speed up the process to save my job, I said, almost as if someone said it for me, "I have changed my mind, and I'm not going to waste your time. This has put so much stress on my family, and I'm not going to live that far from them. I appreciate it, but I'm going to leave the company."

I knew it was over at that point. I bawled my eyes out, and was scared to death for what I had just said. I couldn't even believe I had said it. But still in a place deep down inside, something told me it was right, and it would be okay. Shortly after I had accepted that fact, that God would work it out, is when He did.

That's when I received a call for an interview with a company that wanted to interview me near the beach only three hours away. Now I know once again this was a test. Near the beach? My dream living spot? I was so excited, I asked my now husband to drive me there, and he did. As I mentioned without hesitation, he helped me prep for the interview on the way, and it was the best interview I had ever done in my life. Once again, the high wore off from doing a great job. We sat in silence on the way home knowing we had yet another difficult decision to make. Three hours was better, but not close enough still, and how was I going to turn down living somewhere I could be on the beach in ten minutes after leaving work?

But once again, I was told to say "No, thank you" when the offer came to me. How can I turn down yet another job? I was days away from not being an employee anywhere. For the first time in my life since age fourteen, I wouldn't have any work.

Then my bonus mom said, "Call this woman." That wonderful woman full of God and words and prayers like I had never heard before prayed and thanked God for finding me the job locally just in time before it even happened, declared my situation healed, and I didn't even know her. I was amazed when the same company I had just turned down a job with called me and said, "How about our location near your house in Greensboro?" Just like that, I had my new employer before I was no longer considered an employee at my old job, and a severance payment large enough to buy our house. My salary was almost exactly the same even. God stepped back in and took over once I stepped out in faith. The decision the enemy tried to get me to make was to stay comfortable with the company I spent twelve years at, to leave this wonderful blessing of a husband I had been given, for a life that was more than I could have ever prayed for. Because anything else would be dangerous, and why would I stay for a man when I was skeptical of relationships in the first place? But God.

I'm reminded of all this. I'm also reminded of how when I left controlling the situation of being pregnant, but being told the baby couldn't make it and I would miscarry. Tired of wondering every day what would happen, I relinquished control and said, "God, it's okay if it's not meant to be right now. Please just go ahead and give me my answer." I wrote it down in this book, went to lunch with my son, and that's where it began where I got my answer. It was not yet the time.

Here I am now being reminded to relinquish control of when and if it will happen. And finally just know it will when He wants it to. At the perfect time for our lives, not when my Glow app says it will, not when my mind says it wants to, and just at the perfect time. And if not, it's because it was not supposed to, and we will accept that plan as well.

I was also reminded of the fact that I can be busy and still spend time with Him. In the long run, the time spent will save time elsewhere as I am told the right decisions to make and when to lead me on the path of peace and sound judgment. I don't have to fight to find what I need; it will appear when it needs to. So I will write in the meantime, trying to get my ultimate goal of writing to becoming a writer, because God told me that's who I am, and He already knows it's what I love.

The Obstacle Course
of the Enemy

August 21, 2021

The devil fights hard, doesn't he? That's what I heard the first thing today. As a setback to once again being so overstressed, I am incapable of relaxing. I have to leave this job that I just can't seem to get together, someone's on fire every time I turn around, and once I get them back together and leave for another one, I turn back around to see they're already messing up again. Then I don't have energy or time to work on this business that is costing me money right now instead of making money. I miss my family, but I want another baby, I want to cook again, enjoy cleaning the house again, but have this business going so I can still take care of my family and be financially stable for life. Or at least that's the goals.

All of this so that I can write for God every single day because I love it, and He told me I am a writer, but, God, didn't You tell me to start this business too? Can You help me put hard workers in place of the ones that are quitting each week after training and then I have to start again? Is it a politician, Lord, that is causing these problems? If so, God, can you fix them for us? What's the answer to quiet this world, Lord, and make everyone enjoy life again? When you didn't have to be life-alteringly different to enjoy your life or diagnosed with a disease or overworked to be appreciated, when people just worked and enjoyed weekends with friends and family, it just seems like everyone is too stressed or too tired to enjoy life. So what do I do, Lord?

We pray every day for the politicians. We pray every day over our employees. We take it one day at a time calmly because we have already won the battle.

August 28, 2021

How do you combat the devil?

By seeing, He told me the answer to this question. Experiencing life, you don't always have to rush around and make sure you are doing something great, reading the Bible, or talking to God all alone for hours. If you just look and listen, you will see what to pray for. He told me in a way so many things in one situation.

A fear became reality that my extremely sweet and loving boxer I had for ten years was diagnosed with cancer. In looking at her in this new light, I was concerned now every time she couldn't jump up anymore or had to struggle to get upstairs. Not wanting to see the things that can happen, I figured it was crucial the kids know in case she needs help, so I sat them down.

In having a moment with my kids that I knew would be a sorrow we shared together, I realized I hadn't had many moments like this with my kids in so long. I didn't see things they were going through too. Just having that moment opened up conversations like some of the symptoms they continued to have after COVID-19 that I thought were just mine alone. They shared as well, and I was concerned. It brought me to needing to cook more at night after work which I had neglected so they could get protein, that boys need carbs and shouldn't be on keto too. That one was really struggling to teach the other how to use the tractor, and that Marley, our French bully, really needed structure and training and that I should be praying over all this and for healing in case there's any residual effects from COVID-19 in our bodies, and over Daizy that she won't hurt or suffer over this. And I really meant it and knew God would do it for us.

If I truly believed and did my part, God would hear our prayers. That is maybe what is forgotten the most, our part. In praying over the business and its growth and giving me time to work on it, I heard, "How lucky are you to even try to open a business?" Do you believe me or not?

September 18, 2021

Lord, don't leave me.

This is what I said if I was distracted and I started to hear Him when I was not prepared for it. Because sometimes when I'm asking Him really serious questions, I hear answers. But when I'm not able to react to His words with more questions and a paper and pen, I lose it.

The times I used to have with God that were lengthy allowed me to fully relax, when I could read and write for three to four hours on a Saturday. Now with all my distractions, I feel like I don't have full focus where it should be. Yet, God, in everything I read, it says just ask for it, and it will be yours. And God will make the way.

This is the in between that if I wait, it could be my blessing, or it could kill me in between. Of course, the enemy has to interject somewhere.

I was listening to Keion Henderson last Sunday where he spoke about how long a man in the Bible worked for free for seven years just to marry the woman he truly loved, and then was told after the promise of seven years to work even longer for her. But he did it with pleasure, with pain. It was such a wonderful message because it shows that you may have to be in turmoil while you wait for your blessing. But if you do it with peace and pleasure and faith, you get what you want or deserve!

That peace along the way sometimes is like trying to find a needle in a haystack.

Oddly enough (also known as God's plan!), when things do come together at the right moment, oftentimes people don't recognize or want to admit it was God. I'm in the season where my troubles seem like a joke someone is playing on me, on the way to the things I want for my life and my family's lives, seeing blessings within reach but still feeling like I don't have time to get there. God had led me to Keion Henderson for the first time accidentally for something that wasn't intended for me, which then led me to really enjoy his words, and then at the right moment, he puts out the book *The Shift*. I'm praying for something new and wanted it about three years ago. I did mention already that I am impatient by nature. I'm at the point where I pray to stay away from giving up and being depressed and losing hope, which means you lose faith, and I don't want that at all. I know how this goes. How does this happen?

The book *The Shift* is all about "the mean time" while getting to our destiny. One great example is Moses, and a story I never even knew. Just read Exodus 2:16. It's the perfect example of how someone could have missed a sign down the road of misery and stayed in misery but did the right thing that appeared to be the wrong thing to any bystander, and it was his blessing. How crazy. I think to myself, *Would I save someone if it meant my cover might have been revealed as I'm running from trouble?* But you don't know that it is your blessing right in front of you. So where is it coming for me because I seem to get things late unfortunately, and I don't want to prolong or even miss my blessing.

October 2, 2021

Are you trying to distract me more?

This is what I asked God this morning because it seems the more I want to be with Him or doing works for Him, the more distractions come to my life, and I have to learn once more how to find Him with one more burden in the way. I felt like I had too many to begin with. I have still been reading about shifting through one season into the next, and there's moments where you begin thinking there's no way this is going to work out. Were these just my thoughts and not God's direction? Again, the enemy is making you question yourself.

I know for sure what God told me I would become is possible, and that it would be a dream come true. When things are so difficult or you are scared, you begin to wonder if you are following the right path to get there, or if you had made it sound like the path God wanted you to take because it's what you wanted instead.

For example, I'm sitting on this porch that I love so much and would sit on all morning and look at the scenery, writing about God and what He tells me, remembering He told me I would be a writer one day, clear as day. Instantly when He did, I remembered vividly a part of myself I had long forgotten. Somehow long forgotten. How does that happen? Something that brought so much happiness, joy, creativity, spark, whatever it is that lights you up, you forgot it? For me, it was three things, writing, dancing, and singing.

When I was a kid, I loved writing any kind of writing, thoughts, poems, words, stories. Anything that I could make thoughts sound like an elegant dance with, that's what I wanted to do. I even liked writing essays or reports if they were a topic I could do that with especially, and I forgot all this.

I also used to be asked to sing at every function with my family and friends. At five, I sang in a band with adults, a married couple that were friends with my mom and stepdad, and when they came to town, they'd sing at the Holiday Inn in the evening in their lounge. I guess hotels are different now. I'm not sure I've seen this again in a long time. I barely remember that. But I remember a few things. I remember a red velvet dress, and I remember telling my grandma at the beginning of the show she came to, "Mamaw, I'm going to knock your socks off" in front of the crowd. I also remember repeating the chorus of an Elton John song repeatedly because I forgot the rest of the song.

The seasons changed, and I got older, married young and had kids young, and forgot all these things about myself. I was also told I couldn't do either, and made fun of for those passions I had. God told me I would do my passion again for a living, but here I am on Saturday getting ready to stop writing because I have many other responsibilities. Why?

I'd never heard of Keion Henderson before the first time I listened to one of his sermons, and a coworker gave me his name on a Post-it note to give to someone else. Instead of passing it on to that person, I accidentally kept it myself and took it home. I put it in one of the many books I was reading in a random page, and one morning a while later, I picked up the book, and the Post-it fell on my lap suddenly after I had begun reading for almost an hour. I felt compelled to listen to him, and I did. I was hooked immediately on the way he explained everything. Real and true, as it really is in a way I can relate to in my life now or in the past. I felt as though the chain of actions led me to what I was going for to get to my destiny. To also get us to a place where we have more time and less stress to have a baby and fully enjoy it. I also found the encouragement that God could do any amazing thing in our lives if we let Him.

Putting in for several other jobs to help me do that was getting me nowhere. I have a great résumé. I just didn't understand it. I had once again lost another supervisor, and life is again too stressful to relax, let alone work on being an entrepreneur. I have a lot of money invested in this new venture, so I will need this large income for what I have already done. Did I hear Him correctly, or am I doing myself in? So Keion releases *The Shift*. Right now in my life, yes, this is what I need, my shift.

He speaks how everything shifts when challenged, but those who believe God will work it out, stay the course, and those that let doubt in will invite evil, which takes them on a new course! It is as simple as just knowing no matter what the situation is, God will put it back together for us. If we are willing to go faithfully through the situation knowing this for sure, everything you listen to in Christian songs, reading Christian books, or sermons say just that in many, many ways.

How many horrible situations have you seen someone overcome no matter how big or small? I myself have had situations close in all around me where I felt like there was no escape to one day just be plucked out of it like a stuffed animal the claw got a hold of at an arcade, just like that. So how do I quiet the distractions sent to throw me off course to see if I will faithfully overcome them so that I can?

CHAPTER 22

What Are You Going to Do about It?

October 16, 2021

That's what I heard this morning to thinking about my life and all the things I really wanted in it. I thought about when I was relaxing on the porch when I heard God for one of the first few times, and He asked, "What do you want?" And now He's asking, "What are you going to do about it?"

I then thought about the extent of what I was asking for. The end result I must admit is stout, for God, of course, would be easy, but I was reminded again with what are you going to do about it?

I was reminded that I knew my end game. I was an author with a successful business and a healthy husband and children praising God on Sundays together because we have the time to, that we would take up more than six spaces together on the pew, all loving on one another and one child much smaller than its siblings. My thoughts about what I wanted in my life going from one to the next and a timeline of work flashed in front of me.

I was given the means to attempt entrepreneurship because of how much my stressful job pays me. I've lost people there, and it's been more challenging, but it was necessary for me to build it back up each time. That left me little time to work on a business, but the little moments I have, I have come a long way. Thinking of both of those things alone, it's enough to smother me, but there's more. My husband and I rarely get to spend time together, and when we can, we're always tired. I don't get to do much with my kids, and I can't even remember how passionate I am about my creativity. I feel like it's something I long for but don't have enough time to enjoy anymore. Family wants to see us, but we get one day off together, and it's so valuable. We want more spiritual time and add worries and concerns over disturbed children, a senior, practices, games, and possible infertility. It all adds weight, thinking about loved ones going through challenging situations and never getting to spend time with them.

Life really is a struggle, but it hasn't always been, but what are you doing about it? It's a test, a challenge, a lesson if you let it. Your blessing is on the other side. You hear it all the time. You see many people who got where they wanted to be. If they are truly peaceful and joyful, it's because they passed. You can't pray and do nothing and ask God to put it in your lap. Rest and believe if you work hard and do the right things, love people unconditionally because He says to, don't hurt people emotionally, physically, and always have good intentions, He will take you there.

A heart submitted is a heart committed. Working diligently and joyfully while you wait until you've earned your end result.

October 30, 2021

"Willpower. You're going to write about willpower" is what I heard this morning in my random conversation with God. As I was piecing together my life and how God was going to put it all together so modestly, a thought came to me strong, *What if His way is even better?*

I recently read Prepare for War on visionaries, and a practice where people visualize something repeatedly seeing what they want until it happens, and it does, not knowing exactly what they're tapping into with their minds. It definitely reminded me this morning that it's not my decision, and that those that tried to force their life into what they wanted it to be are actually tapping into evil without knowing it. It's almost like trying to bully God, and even after all this time, I was doing that and not even knowing it. What if I'm holding myself back? Everyone says give it all to God and don't worry, especially the Bible and the words of Jesus. Once again, something not easily done. Why do these things that seem so simple seem so hard in real life? If I calculate how much money I have until next pay, think about everything I owe, Christmas is coming, one child going to college, one needing braces, and how much I've invested in the business. How can you truly not worry and wonder how God will put it back together? And then I think, *Just like the last time.*

What does God truly want?

A heart submitted and a life committed to Him. Which means take it all, I give it to You. I trust and believe You blessed my life beyond my own dreams and visions. I'm Yours. Whatever I go through has a lesson, and everything works together for the good for those who believe in You. This is what God said.

January 17, 2022

Wow, what a difference a few months can make. As I read the words from the last time I wrote, I felt the fear all over again from the things that weighed so heavily on my mind. As I fast-forward to 2022, today, I see God yet again working it out in our life.

We did Christmas just fine. Our oldest son is being considered for a program that will pay 100 percent of his college tuition while paying him to work and while he's in school, and I know God will ensure it happens. We put expensive braces on with a hefty monthly payment I wasn't sure how I was going to make, and suddenly I got a job offer that was the answer to my prayers. Unexpectedly, that would provide for our finances above and beyond what I could have expected and thought would be unrealistic to ask for. I still can't believe it.

If you read to this point, you know the stress my current company has put on my life, and it seemed as though right as it was put together and running smoothly, after almost four years of blood, sweat, and many, many tears, tight shoulders, headaches, and pep talks, picking myself back up and trying even harder, when nothing seemed to be working, after all that, a reward.

Understanding what a blessing looks like they say is having peace about it. Knowing it was meant for you. All the things that would have made one hesitant to leave a place where at least they were comfortable at now, all those things were not in the way this time, and I knew God was blessing me and allowing me to shift out of this season to something that would allow us to continue moving forward with so many things I had begun to question. Just like that, He made a way when I didn't see one.

We are also actively seeking our first investment property with the business because of this financial blessing and confirmation that God is behind us, has seen our hard work, sacrifice, and dedication. Moving forward, when you don't see a way is very difficult, especially with a family. You don't want to cause your family hardship of any kind. Stepping out on faith can sometimes make you wonder.

But believing He will catch you every time you fall or feel that you are nearing an end, you can't see a way out of, keep moving forward knowing your savior sees you, challenges you, grows you, and comes through for you right at the moment you need Him to. He already knows you, what you want, what you need, and when. He just needs you to believe and put one foot in front of the other every day to show Him you're willing to walk in any direction He suddenly points you in for as long as he needs you to be there. In order to discover the wonderful life in front of you that he's always working out for you, carving a path, putting pieces together for, if you just trust and enjoy the present, learn from the challenges today that make you stronger for the next lesson, the next blessing, the next assignment, that leads to the one after that, smile, knowing you are covered, you are protected, you are loved, and cared for every single day!

If you let Him.

I am once again encouraged to continue moving forward and see what He has in store for the future.

In the midst of this blessing, we thought we would once again be blessed with a child. Once again, disappointment came, but because

I know God works to put everything together for the good for those that believe in Him, I am peaceful knowing that it is not yet time. We have more to do, and that blessing will come to us when we are ready and when He knows it's time.

February 10, 2022

Maybe you don't have to try so hard.

This was suddenly etched into my mind so strongly, it could only be the Spirit.

As I sat here with so many anticipations of the things ahead of me, I wasn't even able to relax enough to hear Him for an hour. Distraction everywhere and thoughts of the future in the chapter I just closed of my life that caused me so much stress, yet seemed difficult to break free from once I was released. My last day there was yesterday. The place that half of this book was written about. The place I more than once thought might kill me. Suddenly out as I received what I had prayed for the entire time to get away had come through, and now everyone here seemed so happy, and there was much, much, much less stress.

People I had been very challenged by were now giving me praise for how the place was running, and this was before I gave my notice. People I swore couldn't stand me were now genuinely upset in the things they had said about me pulled on my heart. Hearing that they thought I would support them through everything, calling me mama bear, telling me stories of how I inspired them, they admired me, how I took care of them, and brought them together. The real shocker of all was when I was told, "You have a light about you."

All the times I was drowning, I kept on pushing through, and no matter how aggravated they made me, I still always treated them well and fair, and when I felt like I was going to break, only God held me together where I was and in so many ways. In refilling me in my mind with his promise of everything working together for my good if I believe and keep my mind stayed on Him. If I truly care for people and mimic His love for others, I will stay in His good graces and receive the blessings from Him, but also from His people. How many times have you heard words like this, but you just can't believe it?

God will provide. Storms may come, but when we call Your name, say "Move that mountain," and He will. I am the first to admit that all sounds crazy, but what if it's true? Wow! It can't hurt to try, right? How great would all that be. What if I was diligent, where would it take me? Where has it already brought you with little effort, or where is it taking you because you don't give any effort? Or you quit before it comes into fruition. But because it also says in His time, and when you decide to accept the fact you have to be willing to accept His plans for your life and not your own.

When I was drowning and all but promised another job to get me out and having to pray that if it's in God's plan to let it happen and if not to close the door, I then had to be happy afterward when that door was slammed shut. The glimmer of light came in when the door was cracked that this had to be the blessing I had been waiting for, and then it wasn't. This fake blessing would've gotten me out of my current situation. But I would have left a mess where I was. I would have felt bad for leaving in that moment, changes unfinished, and I would have taken a significant pay cut. But I was desperate. Looking back now, it would have been a horrible decision. So at that moment, I had to pick myself back up, go back to my current situation, keep fighting to get it under control in case I never got to leave and thank God at the same time. No, it is not easy, but what if you don't give up and you do keep believing Him, and know and even thank Him for your next real blessing in advance, knowing He'll make it happen when it should?

I thought, *Okay, let's see what You can do.*

So another year later, almost exactly it seems that everything fell into place and quickly. Continued staffing concerns over and over, feeling like I would start over from square one yet again at every turn, and then suddenly out of nowhere, everything seemed to handle itself all within a month. How is this possible? Suddenly we were fully staffed, and now I was leaving, suddenly the phones rang a lot less, and people were working together and happier!

Suddenly a few harmless conversations with a recruiter was turning into something I may need to think about to an offer that seemed like I was in a dream, something about to be closed again I'm sure was my first thought (or the enemy's). But I will be happy and faithful even if it does. But it didn't this time. I wasn't looking for it, I wasn't desperate to have it, and I didn't have to sacrifice anything at all this time. I had total peace that I was leaving everyone in a better position than when I first walked in the door and had given over 100 percent of my efforts, and that what I was going to would make my life even better.

But now I'm suddenly anxious to start over again and what could go wrong. What if they don't like me? What if I'm not smart enough? What if I mess up? What if it's too difficult? What if my business venture becomes impossible or lost in it, all my hard work gone? What if? What if? What if!

What if I believe He's got me again?

What if I don't have to try so hard?

That's what I heard when I couldn't relax.

What do You mean, God?

What if You just keep doing things when You can, and just believe I'll put it all together for You when it's the right time?

Another time I thought I may not be able to thank God for doing was when my pregnancy failed, when each cycle came month after month after deciding to have the tubal reversal and get a wonderful experience with my husband of having a child together. Now exactly a year and a half ago. I spent almost four years on a very stressful job.

Maybe it will just happen when it's all lined up for it perfectly?

Two years ago just before my reversal, I heard God say, "You need to be baptized before you can be pregnant."

I've literally spent the last two years looking for somewhere I could be baptized to include reaching out to the Lighthouse Church in Texas because of how much I've learned from Pastor Keion Henderson. Of course, I won't just go anywhere. I want it to mean something. My church wasn't even meeting in person when I started trying to be baptized. After getting nowhere, they were suddenly doing water baptism on Easter Sunday this year. What a day to be baptized. The day our savior was raised from the dead.

I don't know what to think about what I heard. But what if I'm just happy and blessed and grateful every day in between?

CHAPTER 23

You Are Turning into Who I Made You to Be

February 27, 2022

That's what I heard when I was having time with God this morning. "You are turning into who I made you to be." As I was doing my routine to begin our discussion, I was standing in the kitchen, heating my neck wrap back up, singing along with Aretha, thanking the Lord with my earbuds, and when I heard myself singing, because of how the words were hitting with tears in my eyes, He showed me on our church stage. First, I laughed and said, "I can't even sing from the other side of the stage at church at all and then also never without crying. Wonder how that will sound on a mic." And then I heard, "You don't think I can do it? Well, you definitely could if you wanted to."

Okay then.

How do you argue with someone that turned water into wine?

Maybe you're becoming who I created you to be.

Every time I think back to who I was before God was first in my life, I cringe.

I had good intentions, but I let a lot of people take me out of character. I did a lot of things I wouldn't today knowing what I know

now. But as a young woman with not much guidance and very few role models, it's the only way I knew to be.

I can really only sum it up as being hard. The more that happened to me, the harder I got. There was definitely still a good soul inside of me, but I'm scared to think if I had continued on that path, it would have eventually been gone. I've forgiven them all, my dad for leaving, my mom for the lack of many things, for the sexual abuse and those with any level of involvement, way too many years of physical abuse and control, along with many bad influences along the way. But I had not yet been led, or had light shed on the fact that I needed to forgive myself.

That felt powerful when it flooded my mind. This is my breakthrough!

In early 2020, the Lord spoke to me that we will have a child after I had been baptized, and for that reason, I've been trying to get baptized ever since. The idea of baptism made me happy to be renewed, but looking back, I was not yet ready. I was frustrated with the fact that no one else felt led to do it. With COVID-19, it seemed impossible.

But now here I am registered for baptism on this Easter Sunday. What an amazing day, and to feel more committed than ever before after many of my prayers coming through all at the same time more than I could have imagined myself.

To have been removed from a toxic work environment, that was a challenge to make it good for those around me every day, to all of a sudden being plucked out just like that and put in a place where faith and love of God is all around me, and to not have to make sacrifices out of the norm for it too. I'm amazed at how my prayers were answered.

But I realize there were so many lessons to be learned before it was my blessing.

For one, knowing how much to appreciate it, but then all the hard lessons already learned when I was responsible for so much, then suddenly being able to be baptized after trying for so long. Just like that, once again I'm reminded, what else can You do?

I am once again intrigued at who You can make me. Things that used to anger me don't anymore. The things that kept me hostage but no longer do, the feelings of love I feel but never used to. The worries I used to have are no longer with me, and when new ones arise, I can give them to you to work out. I no longer feel jealous of anyone because you are making me more beautiful all the time, and in a way that's especially just for me. I'm excited to see who I will be in ten years. But I'm happy to see the slow progress on the way.

One of the best lessons or breakthroughs I ever had was be happy and joyful every day along the way. You can't have joy when you're cursing every day as if you hate it and pray for joyful days. You have to just be joyful knowing it's not yet your time, and find the lessons in today that led you to the blessings of tomorrow. If you force the hand of God, you will get things you are not yet equipped to handle. In most cases, you're still not fully ready by the time you get it, but if He gave it to you, He will be next to you holding you up.

Once again, God, thank you for never leaving me. Please only let me take the steps you have built for me alone.

May 1, 2022

May 1, as I circled that date, I was ashamed of myself, especially after saying about how You never stop working for me. Once again, I find myself a tense mess as I fret about all kinds of things. And because it's been over two months since I've sat like this to talk to Him, I have once again tried to handle everything on my own, and because of this, there is a burn in my neck and these super heavy shoulders. I can't even get comfortable. In my defense, I really have struggled to find where I would have enough time to praise Him like I wanted to. I was still talking to Him, and He was still listening, but I wasn't doing it enough to keep the bad spirits away. You kept working for me though God. A quick old "God, please let this conversation go peacefully." Then shockingly, it was easy. Or "Please, God, let this plane land safely for me and everyone on it," and You did. When I thanked You for waking me up and letting me be mobile, healthy, without ailments, I meant it.

You work every single day for me, and I haven't had a conversation with you in two months. But You are still waiting for me. That's a love only God can provide. I don't deserve it, but as I need You the most when I feel like caving in, You bring me to the center, to You. You literally push me there, and that's just what this hardworking mystical Pisces needs to be reined in.

You place so much in my heart to do, and I know when You mean for them to happen. You will make me so happy, but they always seem so far away, and distraction is getting in the way of our conversations and also ones with those I love right after You.

How can I get that direct line of contact I so badly desire to get to those moments when I'm supposed to? You heard me say Pisces, right? There's so much happening around me, it's like I can't find You in a crowded room sometimes, and it's too loud to hear Your voice, and I get lost. And then all of a sudden, they all disappear, and You're all I can see but just briefly enough to take a few more steps forward. He reminded me of how much I loved to write, and how I would love to be an author, not the other way around. You gave me this wonderful vision of my life on the back porch, letting me write for You, and speak to the world. I was ready when You spoke it I think two or three years ago at this point.

You gave me my interests again in reminding me. You gave me a vision of getting lost in what you were saying, and for Your presence, not something I ever thought of in my own mind. You reminded me by saying it was something I did when I was young and gave up on it. Why do I suddenly miss and love it so much afterward?

You pressed the business on my heart that leads to helping those in need. But there's so much I see, Lord. Where do I start, and what do I set down because I don't have the capacity for it all at the same time?

I am all for putting my trust in You. I am beginning to not trust me, that I hear correctly. I know I have been mistaken many times, and thankfully You dropped a roadblock, but I really want to be obedient. I really want to do the things You want me to do.

What's next, right, Lord?

Pray for God to reveal Himself to You. Okay. Doubt and questioning are normal. It's okay to admit it to your Lord and Savior for answers. As you can see, there can be ups and downs and ebbs and flows in faith. Just talk to Him. He will show and tell you the way when you are lost.

C H A P T E R   2 4

I Know God Will Give Me the Life I've Been Searching For

May 15, 2022

But I also know with whom much is given, much is requested. But in the things I've seen since I first started talking to You and trying to hear You, I've seen things above, what I wanted or expected.

I again can't wait to see what You do, when, and how. If I'm completely honest about the hard things I've been through, they were necessary and taught me really who I am.

I felt strong, getting back up each time, ready to fight the next battle, not just by myself anymore, but He stepped in. In trying to be 100 percent confident He would save me from my situation, He brought me a new attitude each time I wanted to doubt, and I saw what all that can do.

You cross over to now. How did you do that so fast? And why have I never made it to the victory before?

Because I had given up in the past, tried to force the pain or situation to stop on my own time and accord. That never really went too well. Those things were small. He let me put in the work.

But when I cried out, "Okay, I can't do this one on my own, I don't have the power." Then I stuck to listening to any and every word I could to stay on track, getting back up when it didn't go right, just thinking in my head there must be something better ahead. When you see that He provides more, abundantly above, all you could ask for, for real, you are shocked.

It may start small, but when you get to that one time that shocks you, you'll never ever look back.

You will receive rewards for your faith repeatedly.

I had my moment like that, twice at least. Now I am addicted to see what God can do. Okay, so if I jump this next hurdle, depending on You the entire way, letting me know what my next move is, if I ask and listen and I'm faithful along the way, I really can do anything next.

June 25, 2022

When the world takes up so much of your time, of course, mainly work, and you're struggling to ask, listen, and hear, what do you do?

When you long for more time with the Lord and just can't seem to get enough, what do you do?

I have so many sticks in the fire. I'm positive they are all meant for me, but I've lost sight of what comes first at times and where I should apply my efforts the most. I know I can't do everything I want to all at once. Lord, help me with my priorities and where my mind should be heavily focused. Or do I spend what little free time I do have to work on everything a little all at once? I'm confused. I know these things are placed in my life by You.

I don't want to be too busy to hear You, Lord. Please help guide me on my next area of focus, Lord, without sacrificing areas I have no choice but to keep afloat and areas that are the most important to me that I don't want to lose sight of.

Lord, please speak to me today and every day.

I need You.

July 2, 2022

Yes, I'm back sooner this time!

That usually means I'm on the right track, I get lost when I go away for too long. I came back thankfully quick considering we're still in a start-up process at work, and I don't really know everything I'm doing, but I've also been listening on what to do and how to handle it, and it's working. I wish I had learned this much earlier in life, but I felt it kicked in right when it was supposed to because I had to feel some things first.

I eagerly handed a lady all my change today and a Starbucks gift card, because I remembered everyone that willingly helped me out when I was struggling and embarrassed. Not at all to brag about it, but because I felt God put her in front of me when she'd reached a point of disparity and loss of faith in others. Because I can't even begin to understand the blessings He has given to me so that I don't feel that way myself. Because He could change that at any time.

One wrong thing in life and I could lose my job or have a devastating life event. None of us are exempt from this by the way.

Are those asking for help just not listening to Him, or are the judgmental the ones that are making them lose faith and hope?

I sat here this afternoon asking for answers because I think I've been doing what He was asking, but still second-guessing the things I think I have heard to do. I have been led to start many journeys, and even seen glimpses of where those journeys can take me. I have learned a lot, and I'm so ready to get going, but it feels like I'm not moving as fast as I should be.

I was told at the beginning of this spiritual relationship I entered with God that I would be an author, which is something I knew I wanted to be all of my life, but had forgotten. I think about it so often and imagine what my life would be like to cultivate my relationship with God and let Him pour out to people through me. How could I forget? I love to think, I love words, I love Him speaking to me, I love learning and being guided.

It is my dream.

It's like He has reminded me of who I was before I let life knock me down and be mad because I let the world guide me and not Him.

I can't help but wonder, God, were these Your big plans for my life, or what if I made them up and that's why I feel like nothing is happening? I'm not doing and seeing the fruition of what You said, and I am even adding on more dreams on top of other dreams, while I'm feeling like I can't accomplish the other missions You gave me. As I was panicking, doubting that I had made up my own dreams, so God wasn't in them, and that's why I'm failing.

I heard, "Didn't you say you can do all things with Me?

"Didn't I say I'd give you abundantly above all you could ask for?

"Didn't I say you'd have peace?

"Slow down and listen."

All the things I want to do that I could taste on the tip of my tongue, and You want me to slow down?

Once again, I'm reminded of when I try to do things on my own and mess it up like we humans do. So if it means Your plans come true and not mine, then I'm with it. I am absolutely on board. In Your time, not mine. Why do we need to be reminded of this so often?

CHAPTER 25

Reminding Me She Is His and Not Ours

September 4, 2022

I could never repay You, Lord.

How You gave us this wonderful woman to do life with. To have as a wonderful wife to our grandad who loved, honored, and stuck by his side until he passed away just as Your word says.

How You gave us this wonderful mother that cared about her daughters every day of her life just as you wished. This wonderful mother who loved unconditionally.

How You gave us this amazing mamaw that put all of us before herself and was always there when we needed her. This wonderful woman that never stopped taking care of someone in her life.

This wonderful daughter that stood by her parents' side until their last days just as You wished, no matter what.

We thank You, Lord, for all the care she gave us all for our entire lives. We thank You for choosing her to be in our lives. We thank You for all the many, many hugs and kisses she gave us.

How she lit up a room with her goofiness, how she managed to be absolutely gorgeous her entire life.

How her responses were sometimes shocking, how she only had the desire to love and have fun all her life. How she'd never hurt a soul, even if she cussed like a sailor sometimes. How she was so very real.

I admired her independence, her desire to never be a burden to someone else. I admire her love for nature, the sun, and the ocean, plants, solitude, and the ability to go into another dimension through a book.

I watched her, and she is part of who I wanted to be. I thank You, Lord, for our grandaddy and our mamaw.

Because we all took from them characteristics and traits, some good, some bad.

But in a nutshell, fun and caring is who You provided us to lead this family together and, Lord, we are all so thankful for them.

We understand that she is Yours and not ours. So thank You, Lord, for the time You gave us with her.

September 6, 2022

I physically couldn't force my mind to tell my body to move this morning, thinking that I would have to accept that every experience in my life from this point on would have to be done without either one of my grandparents.

Maybe God Is Trying to Tell You Something

February 25, 2023

Maybe God is trying to tell you something?

That's what I heard this morning. As I sat outside in my writing and worship spot, where I haven't been or wrote since September for several reasons, of course, just like life and being busy. But also mourning the death of the woman who raised me and was always there to talk to me, the woman I adored so much. My mamaw was truly one of a kind. She did light up a room, loved hard, and was an absolute blast even up to her last year of life. She left so quickly just like my granddaddy, her husband. None of us were ready for either of them to go home when they did. They both always talked about how much they really liked my father. Yes, the one that was not around, the first man to break my heart as I mentioned earlier in this book. So I finally met him on January 18 this year. They were the first people I thought of and wanted so badly to talk with about my experience and the conversations.

So many things they had told me about he told me about also. He shared the same stories about how he had spent time with my grandparents, had helped my granddad on his job, traveling and setting up facilities, and he shared those stories just the same as they had.

He also shared stories about how difficult my mother had been while they were married, and also when they split. Every story sounded so familiar of her character and what my grandparents had said on the situation. He explained how hard she made it for him to see me and to deal with her.

My heart had been open to this possibility recently from unfortunately seeing women bring good men to the point where they wanted to walk away from their children, not because they didn't want them or love them, but because they needed some peace for their own lives and were just tired of the battle.

I did sense he could have tried a little harder, especially once I became an adult. However, when it's been placed in your head from a young age someone wants nothing to do with you, your heart becomes hard for them too. We talked about a few situations where I wasn't very nice to him and even disrespectful, and I could see how that would also turn you away from wanting to try to have that relationship as well. After we met, I wondered why I had not considered until very recently that he may have a version of the story as well. My mother's versions of almost every situation I was there to experience alongside her were extremely different from what I recalled. Every version of her stories were always so different than anyone's. Of course, she's always been the victim. Everyone knows when she gets something in her mind that it's 100 percent, and there is no persuasion any other way, no matter what you say. Behavior that she still unfortunately has and pays for to this day.

What changed this time when I reached out to him from the last times? I had put my hurt aside to hear him out, to let him know I had matured to a place that I wasn't looking for turmoil or a fight. I didn't have any ill intentions. I'd sent messages in the past that clearly said in between the lines that I'm hurt, and an underlying tone that no matter what you say, I'm going to be on guard and ready to pounce. Who wants that? Of course, the change in my delivery was the suggestion of my voice of reason in the form of my husband who continuously makes me a better person, even if it takes a little persuasion at times. But I am coachable if I trust you and what you're saying makes sense, and as usual, what he said made perfect sense.

It's quite possible God is trying to tell you to change your perspective on something or someone to open your mind and for him to do great work in your life. Sometimes even for great healing. Are you listening, being coachable, or stubborn and hardheaded or hearted. Stop blocking your healing or blessing. Take it from me, I have for many things in my life. I wanted so badly to talk to my grandparents and ask them why didn't you try to tell me to open my heart and mind to the other side of this story and save me some heartache, not all, of course, but some.

One night last week, I had a dream that was so vivid and real that I was speaking to my granddad. It was so real that the entire next day, I kept thinking how great it felt to hear him, but how disappointed I was on the choice of our conversation. It was a repeat of an actual discussion we had after my great-grandmother had passed away, his mother-in-law. I felt the same disappointment in him that I did the first time he told me it was the right time for her to go because she was getting to be too anxious and too much to deal with. I recalled the same reaction I had the first time we had this conversation which was very offended! "Granddad! How can you say that?" As always, he was never moved by my reaction or anyone's reaction for that matter and stuck to his answer of this being the right time. When I discussed this dream with my husband, he said, "Maybe this time the conversation in the message meant something different to you."

Once I thought about it, I realized it did. Timing is everything. Not just timing, but God's timing is crucial. Looking back to all the many things I experienced in my life, I realize I had so many opportunities to become hateful, bitter, to give up, to become hardheaded or hearted. Somehow every lesson was rescued just in time, and I was left with scars that allowed me to be a better person, a better leader, and a more determined, understanding and patient person.

Once God fully stepped in and placed things and people into my life to assist me with the spirit of mercy, grace, and a deep thirst for all things that only God can provide right at the perfect moments, I have truly never been the same. The peace I feel more and more each day is something I could never turn away from trying to get more of each and every day.

This definitely doesn't mean my old ways and feelings and triggers don't raise their heads quite frequently, but I'm reminded more quickly each time they do that someone or something rather is out to get this wonderful gift I have finally found from God that has been here all along, waiting for the perfect time for me to find it.

CONCLUSION

I have been writing this book for the past few years, always wondering if I would get to a place to publish it. After my mamaw passed away in September, I started typing it, a few pages at a time when I could, which wasn't that often because of my schedule. One night at random, because my husband had to stay late at work, I picked up my laptop and my journals and started typing. I had almost talked myself out of it because I started to think this is hopeless. I never have time for it. At this rate, it will never get done, and I'm just wasting my time. Time, I don't get a lot of. Time I could be relaxing, for a change. Instead, I picked it up and began typing. I flipped ahead a few pages to see how many I could get done until the next date I began writing again, and when I did, I felt a wave of encouragement come over me as I realized I only had four pages left to type! I could see the end of something I have worked on for so long and see the possibility of what God had told me in the beginning of this journey coming true. Even if only the possibility, what if I just trust Him yet again?

I pray that these words and thoughts that God has given me over the past few years that have transformed me in my life can help someone else by realizing the truth of what God can do for anyone, no matter what walk of life they are in.

Over the course of these past few years, I have been documenting large challenges in my life, such as the healing of past traumas, losing my career of twelve years that could have ended my relationship with my now husband through separation, a four-year career that challenged me to the fullest extent during the pandemic, losing a child and possibly the experience of having one altogether, the loss of a woman that meant everything to me, and healing enough to meet my father for the first time.

All of these situations had a path that seemed much easier to follow that would have led to disappointment and loneliness, including the doubt and despair that the enemy tried to create in my head in response to God telling me how I can overcome them if I stay faithful. As I began to listen, learn, and create a bond with the Lord, I felt the freedom and peace that comes along with trusting Him and responding to life's challenges as He would want me to. Looking back at the progress I have made and how He has transformed me into someone new that I don't even recognize for the better, my thirst to continue hearing Him and transforming into the version of me He created gets stronger.

I wanted to share with people out there who have been through dark things in their lives or the struggles of normal life that sometimes we don't think we can even handle, I desperately want you to know who and what you can become if you truly allow God into your life.

If God can transform my heart after all the ways life has worked to harden it, He can most certainly do it for anyone. Come with me on this journey to peace, freedom, and love. It's not always easy. It can be a lot of work. I have had to say goodbye to people I loved that hindered my journey along the way, let go of who I used to be, looked inside difficult memories to heal them. The peace I have received in exchange is more than worth it in ways I cannot adequately express. The strength He can provide you in exchange for hurt is amazing.

I am choosing to let Him write my story. Here is my dream, and cheers to watching it come true. Remember, He can do the same for you.

If you let Him.

WHAT IS FAITH?

Faith is confidence in what we hope for and assurance about what we do not see (Hebrews 11:1 NIV).

There are many examples throughout the Bible of those that were provided miracles and victories that should not have been. But God.

They had faith that God would provide and did not doubt or waiver from that faith.

Hebrews 11:6 (NIV) says, "And without faith it is impossible to please God, because anyone who comes to Him must believe that He exists and that He rewards those who earnestly seek Him."

I signed the agreement to publish *If You Let Him* on July 20, 2023, with unanswered prayers and direction to publish it anyway with the faith that those prayers would eventually be answered and the confidence to proclaim this one day away from a deadline to end the pursuit of extending our family but still instructed to publish that our dreams will all come true.

Almost instantaneously after signing, blessing after blessing occurred. Very large miracles began to happen that could only be God in a way that I knew had to be a reward for our faithfulness even during the unknown. I don't know what He will name this next chapter or how He will work it all together for our good, but come along with me to find out as I continue to share the workings of God in our lives. I promise you won't regret it. Life gets sweeter each day you depend on God and see his light grow brighter.

ABOUT THE AUTHOR

Alysia Jackson grew up in the small town of Lancaster, Ohio, where she began working at a very young age, and eventually moved out on her own at the age of seventeen, after only completing eight years of school and not much to her name. Feeling destined to never have the ability to make much of her life due to many challenges and obstacles, through much hard work, determination, and dedication, she was able to gain work experiences and promotions that led her to completing a bachelor's degree while raising two small children in her midtwenties. In 2016, she felt a strong pull on her life to relocate to North Carolina and was selected to do so through her company of employment. Going out on a whim that she now knows is called faith, this is where Alysia eventually found her husband and soulmate, who showed her another way of life than what she was previously used to, including what it truly meant to feel loved and cared for. In helping her heal through past traumas in her life, her husband also piqued her interest in a relationship with God. With the help of her husband and his loving family members, she began to experience a deeper connection to God, His peace, and her purpose in life. She is now inspired to share this amazing connection to God with everyone that's willing to read or listen in hopes for all to experience His love.